ALL ABOUT OUTDOOR STRUCTURES AND FURNITURE

ALL ABOUT OUTDOOR STRUCTURES AND FURNITURE

JOHN BURTON BRIMER

Illustrations by the Author

THEODORE AUDEL & CO.

a division of

HOWARD W. SAMS & CO., INC.

4300 West 62nd Street
Indianapolis, Indiana 46268

PHOTOGRAPH ACKNOWLEDGMENTS:

American Plywood Association: 55, 87, 88, 89 (*bottom*), 91.

Masonite Corporation: 89 (*top*), 90.

California Redwood Association: 28, 31, 49, 52.

Western Wood Products Association: 30 (*top*), 92, 93.

ISBN: 0-672-23820-9

Manufactured in the United States of America

Contents

Build Your Own Outdoor Furniture

With life becoming more informal every day and with outdoor life an accepted part of the American scene, there are many good reasons for building your own furniture. Use it for sitting outdoors, for entertaining on your terrace—take full advantage of all the possible delights offered—and have furniture which is of a different character from that run-of-the-mill stuff one sees so much of today. While there are many kinds of inexpensive outdoor furniture which can be purchased for use on the terrace, some of it rather good in design, there is an increasing need being felt for good *permanent* tables and for seats which are strong and may be left outdoors the year round. Also, with our small quarters and changeable climates, a need for a good *demountable* table has been expressed with frequency.

Therefore we present herein a number of simple designs which almost any amateur craftsman will find easy to construct, for furniture which will add to the joy you take in your garden. Some is modern in character, so it will fit more comfortably with the modern home in good taste than will commercial furniture with its shrieking colors, its machine-made curves and angles. Other pieces will fit well with traditional homes, and several of our designs will integrate with either modern or traditional styles.

One of the main drawbacks to commercial furnishings is the impermanence of the pieces offered. Cheaply constructed, they are so light in weight that they won't last long, are never satisfactory to use, and when the final analysis is made of costs, they prove not to have been so inexpensive after all. The furniture shown here is planned to be able to withstand ordinary weather, so that it can be left outdoors; it need not be whisked under cover at the approach of every storm. It will take its beating from children's (ab)use and still look all right, for its simple, good-looking lines, its rugged character are *designed for use*. And it will age well. If you should ever need to replace any parts for any reason, you will find them either in your wood scrap box or at your nearest building supply house. Can commercial furniture offer this advantage?

SPECIAL FEATURES

Note that the seats and tables we call "demountable" have tops which can be taken off for storage in the garage or cellar during the inclement months, leaving only the masonry parts to bear the brunt of ice and snow during the winter. Those made entirely of cinder blocks and stone slabs can, of course, be left outdoors and used on those few bright days of winter when the sun lures you out for a quick picnic in the sparkling air. These, too, can be called "demountable" because they can be moved from one spot in the garden to another if you wish—from the open terrace into a sun-trap in a corner, from the terrace alongside the house to another place where you may have an outdoor fireplace for cooking.

But they are rather heavy and you won't want to move them too often.

Consider the tables which fold down from a porch or terrace railing and those which lower from a kind of outdoor "breakfront." With one of them you can have a good-looking piece of furniture which does not take up a great deal of space when it is not in use.

In addition to these features you will find a number of designs for seating pieces. Seats can be built in as integral parts of the shelters, and one should not overlook the possibility of considering low walls which may be used as seats, too. These will "come in very handy," as my mother used to say, when you are entertaining the family or large numbers of people on the terrace for luncheon or for cocktail parties, or other gatherings.

The primary consideration in choosing outdoor furniture, whether you build it yourself or buy it, is that it should be practical and useful. Secondarily, it should be good-looking and simple, so that it fits well into its surroundings and is a part of the general picture—an unobtrusive part. You will find that the natural qualities of unfinished wood, stone, and building blocks used for furniture will help to keep it in the background and in harmony with the house and natural parts of the garden. If the materials must be painted, we urge that soft colors be employed— never bright or dominant ones, *never* hard reds or bright oranges, or even that unnatural green one so often encounters.

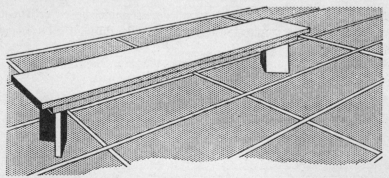

BENCH—PORTABLE OR PERMANENT

A bench of simple lInes, built of sturdy 2″ stock and painted to harmonize with the house or stained a dark, woodsy color, will be a useful addition to any terrace. If you wish to place it permanently, treat the posts with wood preservative, set them in concrete beside the terrace or in whatever location you have chosen for the bench to be placed.

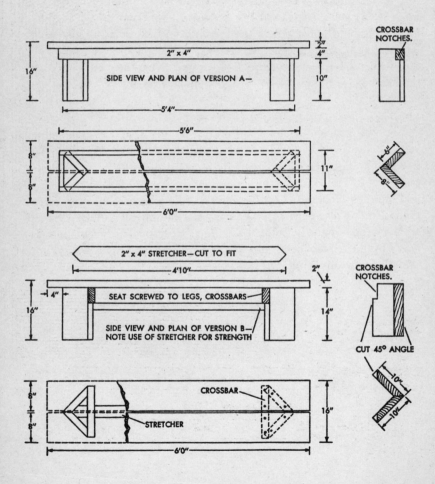

BENCH FOR GOOD COMPANIONS

Backless garden benches are coming more and more into use. This bench can be used alone as shown in the bottom version, or can be used to angle off to follow a terrace boundary or one of the part-shade, part-sun trellisses now so popular. It will adapt itself to any site and can be portable or permanent. Built of 1" x 2" x 2" blocks it has apron boards and two center boards of 1' x 6" shaped at ends to meet end aprons of 1" x 4" stock. Supports consist of two 2" x 8"s shaped as shown resting on 2" x 4" feet which protect them from rot. (Permanent version is set in concrete after treatment with a wood preservative.) Note that boards are butted at corners, nailed or screwed together securely, as center blocks are, also.

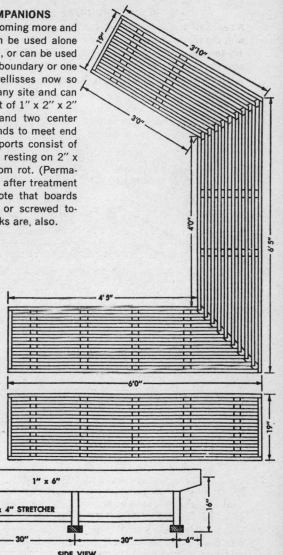

NOTE: Fit boards at angles first, then cut at ends for proper fitting, ease of construction, less wood waste.

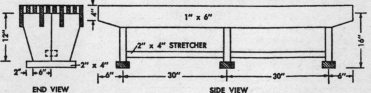

END VIEW

SIDE VIEW

1" x 6"

2" x 4" STRETCHER

2" x 4"

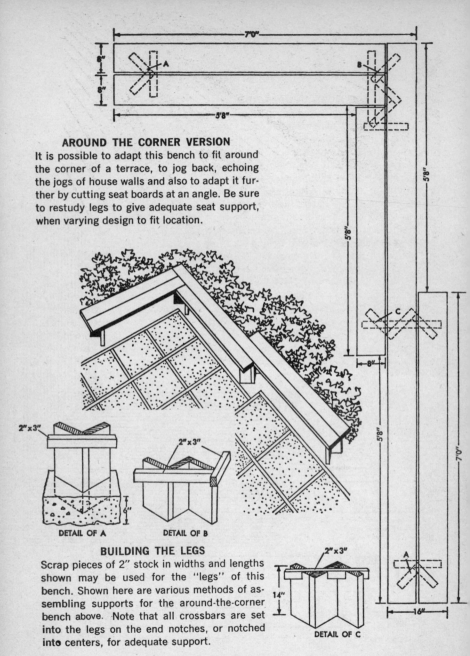

AROUND THE CORNER VERSION

It is possible to adapt this bench to fit around the corner of a terrace, to jog back, echoing the jogs of house walls and also to adapt it further by cutting seat boards at an angle. Be sure to restudy legs to give adequate seat support, when varying design to fit location.

DETAIL OF A

DETAIL OF B

BUILDING THE LEGS

Scrap pieces of 2" stock in widths and lengths shown may be used for the "legs" of this bench. Shown here are various methods of assembling supports for the around-the-corner bench above. Note that all crossbars are set into the legs on the end notches, or notched into centers, for adequate support.

DETAIL OF C

FOLDAWAY TABLE ON A BALUSTRADE OR WALL

A table which folds away when not in use, leaving precious terrace space free, is an asset to be prized. Hinges attach the 2″ x 2″ frame to balustrade, fence or wall; hinged legs fold up inside frame to be held by turn-buttons on a stationary block. Legs are secured by a $\frac{1}{4}$″ steel rod bent into a double hook, fitted into holes bored in leg and frame. Use $\frac{1}{2}$″ outdoor plywood for table top and for legs, too, if desired. Vary the dimensions to suit your needs. This table will seat five adults with good elbowroom.

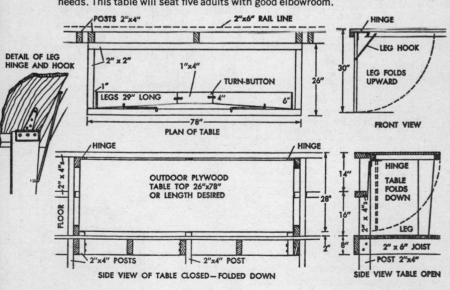

FOLDAWAY DEMOUNTABLE TABLE

For winter storage, take off the table top made of 1″ x 6″ boards mounted on 2″ x 4″ frame, which fits over leg and stretcher construction. A long pivot bolt permits folding up for carting and storage. Rot-block feet may be replaced as necessary. Table top stays on by own weight if frame is carefully fitted to legs. Vary top size to suit needs.

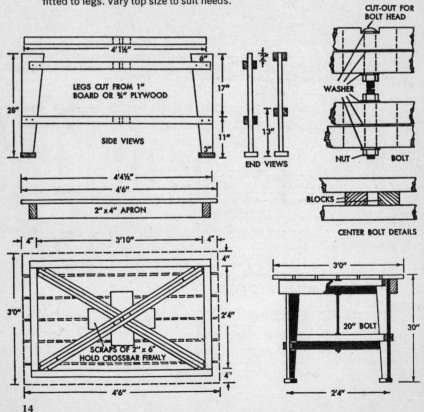

4′1½″
6″
LEGS CUT FROM 1″ BOARD OR ¾″ PLYWOOD
17″
28″
11″
3″
SIDE VIEWS

END VIEWS
13″

CUT-OUT FOR BOLT HEAD
WASHER
NUT   BOLT

4′4½″
4′6″
2″ x 4″ APRON

BLOCKS
CENTER BOLT DETAILS

4″   3′10″   4″
4″
3′0″
2′4″
20″ BOLT
30″
2′4″
SCRAPS OF 2″ x 6″ HOLD CROSSBAR FIRMLY
4″
4′6″

FOLDING LOVESEAT OR BENCH FOR THE TERRACE

A chair and a loveseat of similar design are easy to build, easy to fold up and take in for the winter or for quick shelter from a summer shower. The boards used for seats may be $\frac{5}{4}''$ or 2'' (the lighter weight may make them more transportable) with 1'' x 4'' stock used for backrest boards. Legs may be cut from 2'' x 10''s or heavy outdoor plywood.

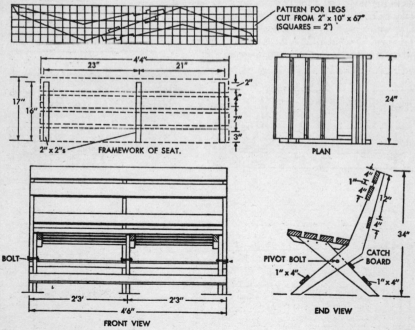

PATTERN FOR LEGS
CUT FROM 2" x 10" x 67"
(SQUARES = 2")

23"   4'4"   21"

17"   16"   2"   4"   7"   3"

2" x 2"s   FRAMEWORK OF SEAT.

24"

PLAN

4"   1"   4"   12"   34"

PIVOT BOLT   CATCH BOARD

1" x 4"   1" x 4"

END VIEW

BOLT

2'3'   2'3"

4'6"

FRONT VIEW

LARGE COFFEE TABLE FOR OUTDOORS

For informal lunches, suppers and for snacks at any time a large coffee table built of outdoor plywood, protected by wood preservative, and painted in a gay color is a good solution. This one may be made as shown in the sketch, with shaped apron and the corner "legs" cut out, too, or it may be made perfectly wedge shaped as in the sketches of the parts below. The feet may be changed, should they decay from contact with moisture, waste blocks being used for them. Or if the table is used on a porch where it is dry the feet may be dispensed with.

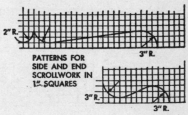

3'6" x 6'0"

5" R.

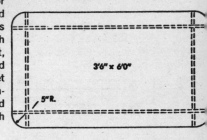

PATTERNS FOR SIDE AND END SCROLLWORK IN 1" SQUARES

2" R.   3" R.

3" R.   3" R.

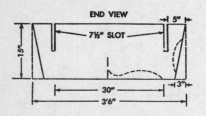

END VIEW

5"

7½" SLOT

15"

30"

3"

3'6"

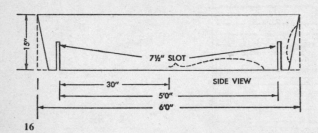

SIDE VIEW

15"

7½" SLOT

30"

5'0"

6'0"

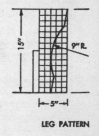

LEG PATTERN

15"

9" R.

5"

CUPBOARD WITH LET-DOWN TABLE

When a garden house or terrace has limited space, the need is acute for a dining table which will fold away. This table, combining storage space for plates and other necessary equipment, is hinged to let down, the rear resting on the jutting lower cupboard space, the front supported by a hinged leg which is a part of the decorative frame when not in use. Potted plants grace the shelves on either side. Lower cupboards may have two doors to divide into center and two side compartments.

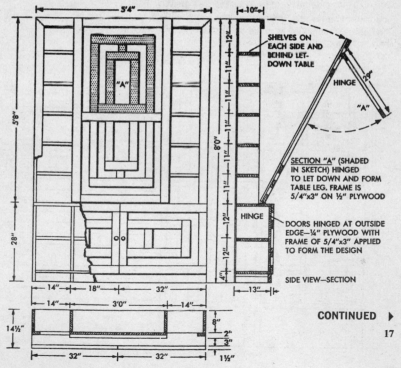

SHELVES ON EACH SIDE AND BEHIND LET-DOWN TABLE

HINGE

"A"

SECTION "A" (SHADED IN SKETCH) HINGED TO LET DOWN AND FORM TABLE LEG. FRAME IS 5/4"x3" ON ½" PLYWOOD

HINGE

DOORS HINGED AT OUTSIDE EDGE—¼" PLYWOOD WITH FRAME OF 5/4"x3" APPLIED TO FORM THE DESIGN

SIDE VIEW—SECTION

CONTINUED ▶

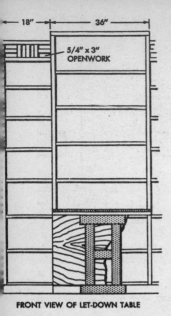

FRONT VIEW OF LET-DOWN TABLE

5/4" x 3" OPENWORK

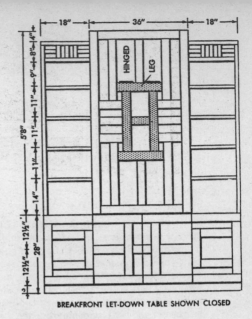

BREAKFRONT LET-DOWN TABLE SHOWN CLOSED

HINGED LEG

PRIVACY FENCE WITH LET-DOWN TABLE

Fence table has no lower compartment, only 2" x 6" shelves behind table which continue alongside to make open shelves for plants, etc. Vary cupboard and table dimensions to suit.

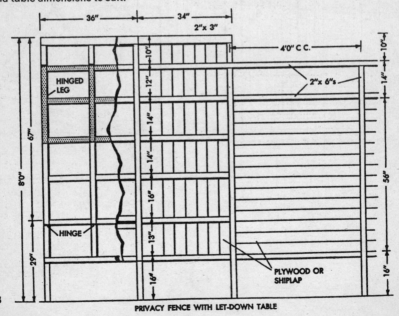

HINGED LEG

HINGE

2" x 3"

4'0" C.C.

2" x 6"s

PLYWOOD OR SHIPLAP

PRIVACY FENCE WITH LET-DOWN TABLE

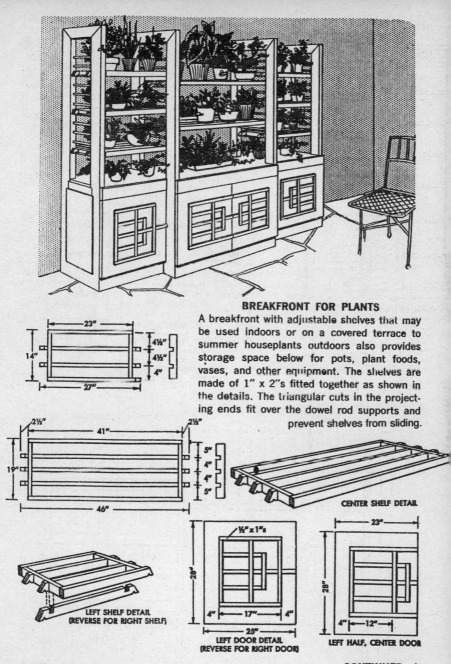

BREAKFRONT FOR PLANTS

A breakfront with adjustable shelves that may be used indoors or on a covered terrace to summer houseplants outdoors also provides storage space below for pots, plant foods, vases, and other equipment. The shelves are made of 1" x 2"s fitted together as shown in the details. The triangular cuts in the projecting ends fit over the dowel rod supports and prevent shelves from sliding.

CENTER SHELF DETAIL

LEFT SHELF DETAIL
(REVERSE FOR RIGHT SHELF)

LEFT DOOR DETAIL
(REVERSE FOR RIGHT DOOR)

LEFT HALF, CENTER DOOR

CONTINUED ▶

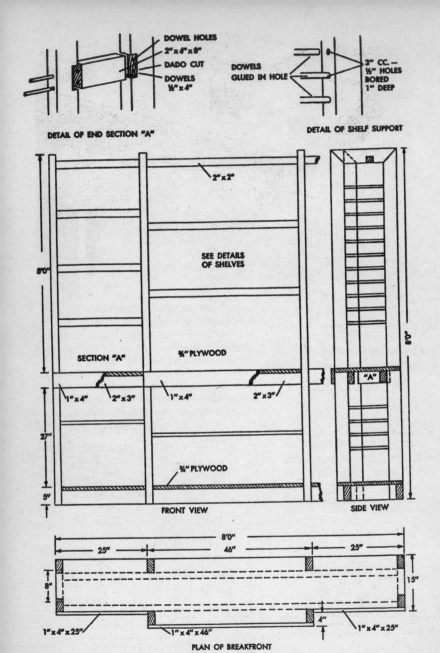

DOWEL HOLES
2" x 4" x 8"
DADO CUT
DOWELS
½" x 4"

DOWELS
GLUED IN HOLE

3" CC. —
½" HOLES
BORED
1" DEEP

DETAIL OF END SECTION "A"

DETAIL OF SHELF SUPPORT

2" x 2"

SEE DETAILS
OF SHELVES

8'0"

SECTION "A"

¾" PLYWOOD

1" x 4"   2" x 3"   1" x 4"   2" x 3"

"A"

27"

¾" PLYWOOD

5"

FRONT VIEW

SIDE VIEW

8'0"

8'0"

25"   46"   25"

15"

8"

1" x 4" x 25"   1" x 4" x 46"   4"   1" x 4" x 25"

PLAN OF BREAKFRONT

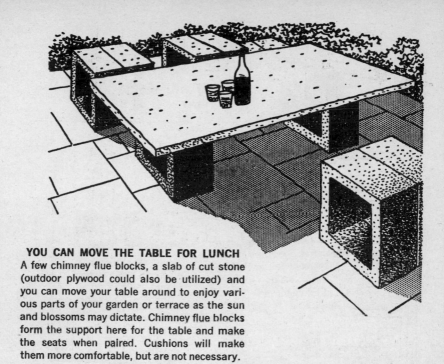

YOU CAN MOVE THE TABLE FOR LUNCH

A few chimney flue blocks, a slab of cut stone (outdoor plywood could also be utilized) and you can move your table around to enjoy various parts of your garden or terrace as the sun and blossoms may dictate. Chimney flue blocks form the support here for the table and make the seats when paired. Cushions will make them more comfortable, but are not necessary.

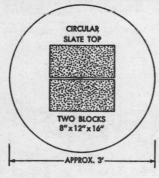

CIRCULAR SLATE TOP

TWO BLOCKS 8" x 12" x 16"

APPROX. 3'

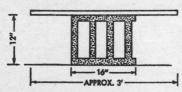

12"

16"

APPROX. 3'

COFFEE TABLE OF BLOCKS AND SLATE

A slate top cut round or in irregular slab style set on a pair of wall blocks makes a most acceptable low cocktail or coffee table. It can be easily picked up and moved, and because it is impervious to weather can be left out all winter as a bird feeding table.

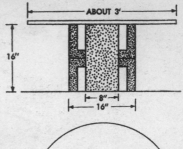

SLATE COFFEE TABLE

In most sections it is possible to buy a slate top cut in a circle. The table shown here is either demountable or permanent and the supports are simple to assemble. A pair of half flue blocks are stacked as shown inside a full square chimney flue block. If you want to make them permanent, mortar them on a secure foundation, mortar the slate top securely in the center, and your table is done.

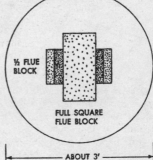

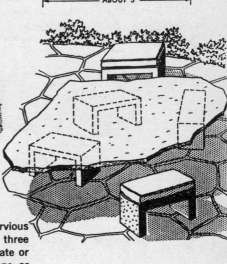

TWO INFORMAL TABLES

A table which is demountable yet is impervious to weather can be built by stacking up three chimney blocks and placing a slab of slate or other stone on top. It may be cut stone or irregular in shape as shown above. Or, by using several half-blocks placed to support the slab, a larger piece may be used for a low table. Half blocks with cushions made to fit make low seats for terrace use.

DEMOUNTABLE PLYWOOD AND BLOCK FURNITURE

An outdoor plywood top screwed to a simple framework which fits around a pedestal of cement blocks mortared to a concrete foundation makes a most useful outdoor dining table. Benches on block supports are also sturdy, simple and good looking, built of planks on a framework which also fits around blocks. Note that both the table and bench tops may be removed and taken indoors for storage or for winter protection.

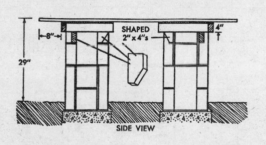

SIDE VIEW

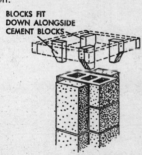

BLOCKS FIT DOWN ALONGSIDE CEMENT BLOCKS

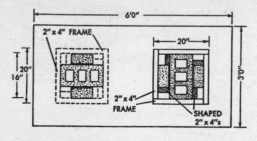

PLAN

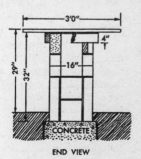

END VIEW

CONTINUED ▶

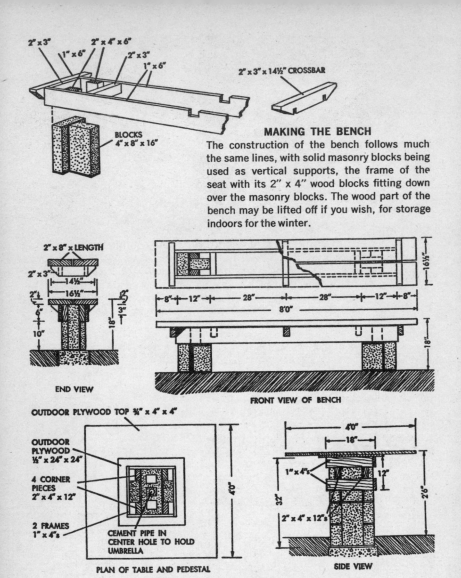

2" x 3"
1" x 6"
2" x 4" x 6"
2" x 3"
1" x 6"

2" x 3" x 14½" CROSSBAR

BLOCKS
4" x 8" x 16"

MAKING THE BENCH

The construction of the bench follows much the same lines, with solid masonry blocks being used as vertical supports, the frame of the seat with its 2" x 4" wood blocks fitting down over the masonry blocks. The wood part of the bench may be lifted off if you wish, for storage indoors for the winter.

2" x 8" x LENGTH
2" x 3"
14½"
16½"
2"
6"
10"
18"
2"
3"
16½"

END VIEW

8" 12" 28" 28" 12" 8"
8'0"
18"

FRONT VIEW OF BENCH

OUTDOOR PLYWOOD TOP ¾" x 4" x 4"

OUTDOOR PLYWOOD ½" x 24" x 24"

4 CORNER PIECES 2" x 4" x 12"

2 FRAMES 1" x 4"s

CEMENT PIPE IN CENTER HOLE TO HOLD UMBRELLA

PLAN OF TABLE AND PEDESTAL

4'0"
16"
1" x 4"s
12"
32"
2" x 4" x 12"s
2'6"

SIDE VIEW

A DEMOUNTABLE SQUARE TABLE

A square table built of outdoor plywood fits on a single pedestal of cinder or concrete blocks. To keep it solid and stable, longer wooden blocks and a double banding of wooden strips are used to fit down around the masonry pedestal. Screw a 24" square of plywood to the top of the framework, then mount plywood and framework to table top with aluminum screws, thus avoiding holes in the top surface of the table. One-by-three stock can be used to frame under table edges for strengthening it, if you should wish to do so.

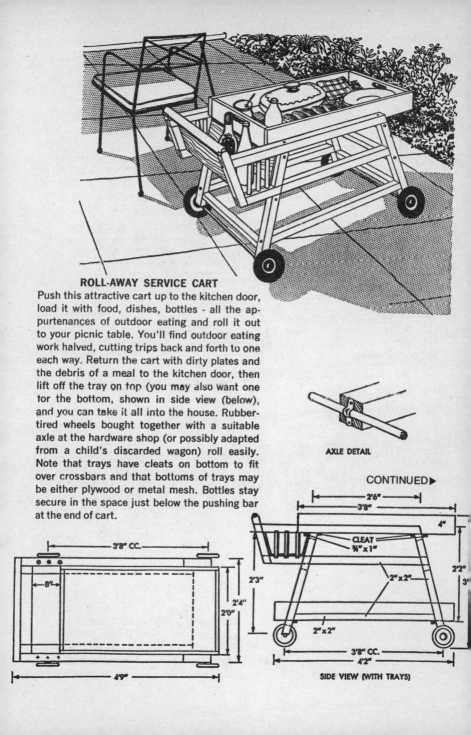

ROLL-AWAY SERVICE CART

Push this attractive cart up to the kitchen door, load it with food, dishes, bottles - all the appurtenances of outdoor eating and roll it out to your picnic table. You'll find outdoor eating work halved, cutting trips back and forth to one each way. Return the cart with dirty plates and the debris of a meal to the kitchen door, then lift off the tray on top (you may also want one for the bottom, shown in side view (below), and you can take it all into the house. Rubber-tired wheels bought together with a suitable axle at the hardware shop (or possibly adapted from a child's discarded wagon) roll easily. Note that trays have cleats on bottom to fit over crossbars and that bottoms of trays may be either plywood or metal mesh. Bottles stay secure in the space just below the pushing bar at the end of cart.

AXLE DETAIL

CONTINUED▶

SIDE VIEW (WITH TRAYS)

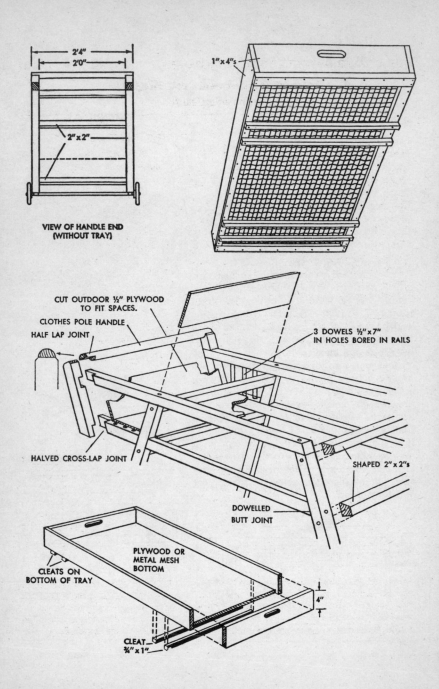

2'4"

2'0"

2" x 2"

VIEW OF HANDLE END
(WITHOUT TRAY)

1" x 4"s

CUT OUTDOOR ½" PLYWOOD
TO FIT SPACES.

CLOTHES POLE HANDLE

HALF LAP JOINT

3 DOWELS ½" x 7"
IN HOLES BORED IN RAILS

HALVED CROSS-LAP JOINT

SHAPED 2" x 2"s

DOWELLED
BUTT JOINT

PLYWOOD OR
METAL MESH
BOTTOM

CLEATS ON
BOTTOM OF TRAY

4"

CLEAT
¾" x 1"

Table of Measurements and Heights:
Furniture for Adults

SEATS:	HEIGHT
Floor to seat	16"–18"
Floor to shoulder rest	36"–37"
Seat to head clearance	2' 11" min.
Width, side to side, minimum	15"
Depth, back to front, minimum	15"
Clearance, top of seat to table	11"
Clearance, top of knee to table	5"
Clearance, seated people, elbow to elbow	27" min.
Clearance, kick space from stationary seat to table upright	19"–20"
Clearance, space in front of knee	7" plus 12" foot-space
Clearance behind heel, legs vertical	7"
Stationary seats should extend no more than 2"-3" under table line.	

TABLES:	
Width, table used one side only	22"–24" min.
Width, table used on both sides	28"–20" min.
Table height, top to floor	29"
Clearance for knees, seated, min. height	24"
Clearance for seated people, elbow to elbow	2' 3" min.

Children's Furniture Heights

Height of Child	Seat Height	Table Height
3' 3"	1'	1' 10"
4' 0"	1' 2"	2' 1"
4' 4"	1' 3"	2' 2½"
4' 8"	1' 4"	2' 4"
5' 0"	1' 5"	2' 5"
5' 4"	1' 5"	2' 5"
5' 6" and over	1' 6"	2' 5"

NOTE: All the above measurements can be varied to suit the uses of the child and the adult. If you want to experiment to find out what is the best height for you, measure various tables and sitting pieces in your home, using the measurements of those pieces you find most comfortable. The above chart was compiled on the basis of average measurements: that is, tall- to average-sized people.

POTTING BENCHES

Although perhaps potting benches are not strictly furniture, they are a part of the garden picture, and the ones we show here can also be built into basements, garages, or tool sheds. The rolling potting bench will be trundled out on the terrace frequently, so it may be included as a part of the furniture section.

Every gardener has difficulty with storage—where to put stakes, where to put hand tools and all the various useful things which make such clutter when left about the house or garage or out in the garden. These benches will help to organize things and make them orderly and useful. For the indoor gardener, a potting bench is the answer to a prayer when it has storage bins for soil, peatmoss, sand, etc., lots of shelves, and plenty of storage space for pots. Outdoors, too, where people are using more potted plants to get quick color, such a potting bench with a shelter built over it will be most welcome in many a garden.

An odd corner behind a curving fence is put to good use as a potting bench. The trellis from the opposite side is extended over the waist-high 2" x 4"s that form the counter. Large boxes below this contain soil, peatmoss and sand for use in potting up.

With this section, as we have urged for other sections, we suggest that you look at our designs and, if they do not exactly meet your needs, adapt them as you see fit. Change merely for the sake of change is not what we mean, of course, but change for improving the use of the piece so that it adapts to fit your specific needs will give you a taste of the creative experience which is one of the most satisfying joys of craftsmanship. Your furniture can express *you* as much as any other part of the garden does.

A workmanlike potting bench provides a potting surface, adequate bins for soil, sand and peatmoss, shelves for pots and other needs. Exterior-type plywood is used in $\frac{3}{4}$" thickness, mounted on a sturdy framework of bolted 2" x 4"s. Note guards on top and sides.

A permanent bench seating several has back members attached to pergola columns for stability. Framework of 2" x 6"s takes cue for angle cuts from slant of back, echoes it in front. Seat and back are made of spaced 2" x 4"s. Paint bench to match pergolas.

Portable painted bench has a seat formed of three 2" x 8"s screwed to a 2" x 6" crossbar and supported by three 2" x 8" legs that are overlapped 2 inches each side of center space. Note how legs are angle-cut for tight fit, how crossbar is beveled to meet leg line.

A curved seat is supported at ends by bolted multiple 2" x 4"s with others flat against the curving back at the corners. Sabersaw a hefty wide plank in the desired curve, place the two straight sides together and attach them to end cleats fastened to end supports.

A bench may be used for sitting or to display a bonsai tree. Made of redwood—2" x 8" planks for seat, invisibly attached with epoxy-glued dowels set in holes bored in seat plants and in crossbars that, like legs, are 4" x 4"s. Dado crossbars $1\frac{1}{2}$" into legs.

A PLACE FOR EVERYTHING

It's always easier to put a tool back when you've finished using it if there is really a place to put it. This simple pegboard arrangement adapts to the tools you now have, can be adjusted to those acquired later. Work tables for potting, etc., are built above shelves for pots and garden equipment. Table sides are put to work as storage for stakes and hose. Note upper shelves for dusts and sprays. Garbage cans provide covered storage for soil, sand and peatmoss gardeners need for use in pots, flats.

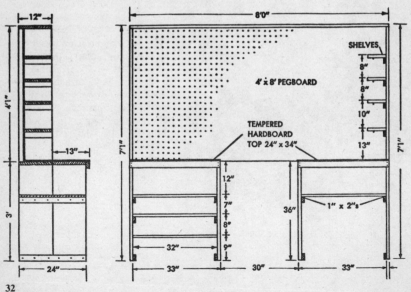

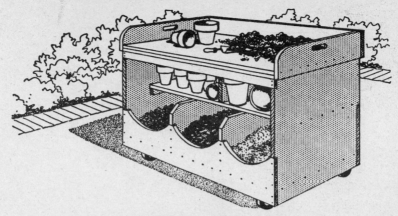

PUSHAROUND POTTING BENCH

Sometimes it is most convenient to have a portable potting bench which can be pushed from one area to another and also be easily stored when not in use. The removable tray on top makes it still more portable—for a small garden perhaps the tray would be sufficient. Peatmoss, sand and soil are stored in the bins below, pots kept on the shelf. Note that the outer parts are made of plywood, the frame and caster supports are of 2" x 4" stock. If desired, use tempered hardboard for topping the bench and tray.

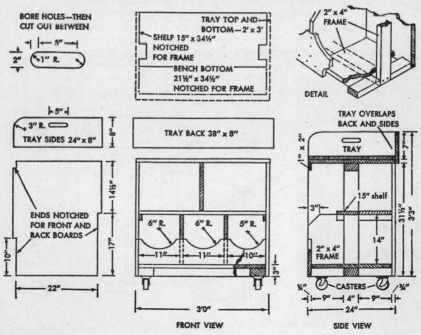

BORE HOLES—THEN
CUT OUT BETWEEN

5"

2" 1" R.

TRAY TOP AND BOTTOM—2' x 3'
SHELF 15" x 34½" NOTCHED FOR FRAME
BENCH BOTTOM 21½" x 34½" NOTCHED FOR FRAME

2" x 4" FRAME

DETAIL

5"

3" R.
TRAY SIDES 24" x 8"

8"

TRAY BACK 38" x 8"

TRAY OVERLAPS BACK AND SIDES

1" x 2"

TRAY

7"

ENDS NOTCHED FOR FRONT AND BACK BOARDS

14½"

17"

15" shelf

3"

31¼"
3'3"

6" R.   6" R.   5" R.

14"

10"

11"   11"   10"

2" x 4" FRAME

22"

3½"

¼"   CASTERS   ¾"

9"   4"   9"

3'0"

24"

FRONT VIEW

SIDE VIEW

A POTTING BENCH WITH MANY OTHER USES

Gardeners fortunate enough to possess greenhouses or those who garden on a fairly large scale outdoors will have need for a potting bench that is sizeable. This one also provides storage bins for peatmoss, potting soil, sand, and has shelves for pot storage and for insecticides, fertilizers, etc. The top is made of hardboard, outdoor quality, which wears well and is relatively impervious to water. Bench may be used for other purposes in between its uses as potting bench, for cutting and arranging flowers, as an auxiliary carpentry bench and in many other ways. The collar around the back and sides prevents soil and debris from falling off, permits putting ingredients of potting soil in a corner for mixing. Note, too, that as the contents of the bins lower from use, front boards may be removed to facilitate remainders being reached. Adapt this bench to a smaller size if you wish, to fit your space, and alter it to suit your own specific needs.

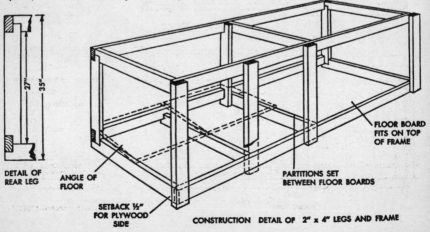

DETAIL OF REAR LEG

ANGLE OF FLOOR

27"   35"

SETBACK ½" FOR PLYWOOD SIDE

PARTITIONS SET BETWEEN FLOOR BOARDS

FLOOR BOARD FITS ON TOP OF FRAME

CONSTRUCTION DETAIL OF 2" x 4" LEGS AND FRAME

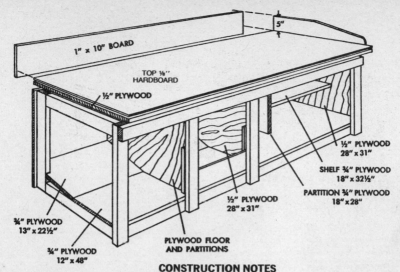

1" x 10" BOARD

5"

TOP ⅛" HARDBOARD

½" PLYWOOD

½" PLYWOOD
28" x 31"

SHELF ¾" PLYWOOD
18" x 32½"

PARTITION ¾" PLYWOOD
18" x 28"

½" PLYWOOD
28" x 31"

¾" PLYWOOD
13" x 22½"

¾" PLYWOOD
12" x 48"

PLYWOOD FLOOR
AND PARTITIONS

CONSTRUCTION NOTES

Note how bottoms of bins are inclined, to throw soil, etc. toward front of bench. Bins may be lined with aluminum or other sheet metal to permit storage of damp materials, if desired, and top may also be finished with metal instead of hardboard. Outdoor plywood in ¾" or ½" thickness is shown, but boards of various widths may be used instead, if top is covered and bins are lined.

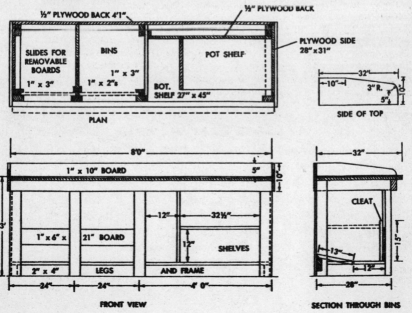

½" PLYWOOD BACK 4'1"

½" PLYWOOD BACK

SLIDES FOR
REMOVABLE
BOARDS
1" x 3"

BINS
1" x 3"
1" x 2⅝"

POT SHELF

BOT.
SHELF 27" x 45"

PLYWOOD SIDE
28" x 31"

PLAN

32"

10"

3" R.

5"

SIDE OF TOP

8'0"

1" x 10" BOARD

5"

10"

3'

1" x 6" x   21" BOARD

12"

32½"

12"

SHELVES

2" x 4"   LEGS   AND FRAME

24"   24"   4' 0"

FRONT VIEW

32"

CLEAT

15"

13"

12"

28"

SECTION THROUGH BINS

2

Little Projects

We present a number of small projects which will not take much time to build, or very much in the way of material, either. They will serve, we hope, as a good introduction to craftsmanship for beginners. More advanced workers will also be interested in them because they are all useful and beautiful in their way—objects which one can make to use for one's own garden or build as gifts for friends who love their gardens.

The plant-stands and outdoor shelves for summering houseplants on the terrace are practical solutions to an everpresent problem of the indoor gardener. Whether they are the very simple demountable ones or more permanent types, they will assist the gardener to keep his plants in good order during their summer vacation outdoors.

The plant shield shown can probably be adapted to many more uses than those shown here. Every gardener recognizes the need for shielding tender plants from the winter sun and cold blasts of wind. By using a decorative shield (something more pleasant to look at out the window than the torn and ragged strips of sagging burlap sacking one usually sees), the sad winter landscape can be made more appealing. Such shields can be painted any color you wish, making them distinct assets rather than bitter necessities when they are installed in your garden.

The cold frame is another project which may be built with very little tool experience. We recommend buying the glass sash rather than making it—sash is cheap and making it is rather an intricate job—and then constructing the cold frame to fit the sash. Advanced workers may wish to go a step further and build the sash. There are many changes which can be rung on the construction of the frame. Permanent sides of brick, concrete, or other masonry may be used, or a wooden frame made to fit over the top to hold the sash. For using such a frame as a hot bed, permanent masonry sides are recommended because of high temperatures and humidity which may rot the wooden sides of the type we show.

Our "Ever Blooming Plant Box" can be adapted to whatever sizes of pots you wish to use in it, and may be built with or without the trellis shown. It will make a bright spot of color beside your front door, on the terrace, or wherever you finally decide to use it. By fitting it with wheels, you'll be able to move it about from spot to spot, changing it about each day or each week, or whenever you give a party.

The "Ugly Duckling Doors" also require but little skill and only a bit of patience for their rebirth and refurbishment. Old cracked panels and odd, mismatched doors can be made into smart, fresh ones and will last many years when they are covered and brought up to date this way.

These, then, are our Little Projects, which we hope will inspire you to find fun in building and will give you many years of pleasure and profit from their use when they are completed.

May all your Little Projects become big ones as your skill and confidence grow.

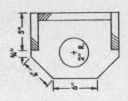

A GARDEN SHRINE

Light enough to be hung on a fence, yet of sturdy enough construction to stand by itself, this little shrine will add interest to the garden. Shown here is a reproduction of a plaque of St. Fiacre, the patron saint of gardeners; the box at his feet will hold either flowers or green vines At left below and at right are shown two versions of the shrine. At left is a pot pocket with holes bored in the bottom for drainage. At right is the version shown in the top illustration with a hole cut in the bottom to admit a pot of flowers. Version at left has pocket fastened to back and has short side pieces screwed to pocket. Plaque hangs on hook.

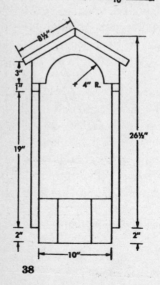

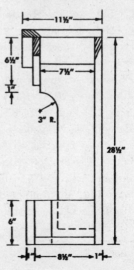

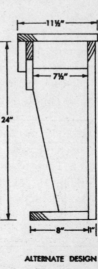

38

ALTERNATE DESIGN

SHOW-OFF FOR POTTED PLANTS ON THE TERRACE

Either houseplants or potted plants prepared for terrace use outdoors will find graduated shelves like these the best possible way to make their contribution. Note the alternate methods of making the shelves, with wooden gratings to allow circulation of air and good drainage. Use either bolts or dowels to hold shelves in place, decorate with trellis slats.

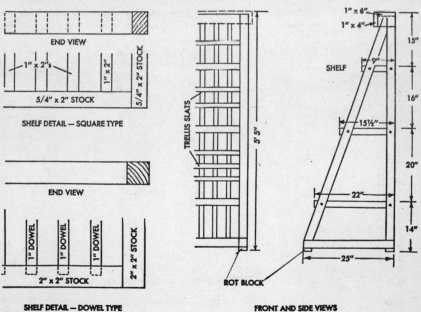

END VIEW

1" x 2"s   1" x 2"

5/4" x 2" STOCK   5/4" x 2" STOCK

SHELF DETAIL — SQUARE TYPE

END VIEW

1" DOWEL   1" DOWEL   1" DOWEL

2" x 2" STOCK   2" x 2" STOCK

SHELF DETAIL — DOWEL TYPE

TRELLIS SLATS

5' 5"

ROT BLOCK

1" x 6"
1" x 4"   15"

SHELF   9"

16"

15½"

20"

22"

14"

25"

FRONT AND SIDE VIEWS

VACATION SPOT FOR HOUSE PLANTS

If you have a few steps down from a north door of your house, you have an ideal spot for summering your houseplants. Build steps of outdoor plywood to match stairs, topping them with wooden gratings so that plants can drain easily. Plant steps are easily transportable for winter storage because all of the gratings are removable. Use a wood preservative and give all wood three coats of paint. Note "rot blocks" which are replaceable.

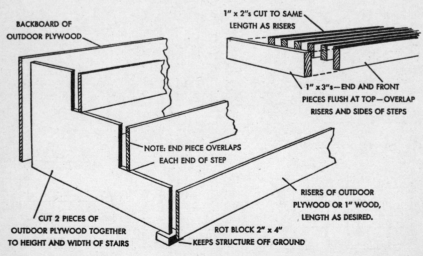

BACKBOARD OF
OUTDOOR PLYWOOD

1" x 2"s CUT TO SAME
LENGTH AS RISERS

1" x 3"s—END AND FRONT
PIECES FLUSH AT TOP—OVERLAP
RISERS AND SIDES OF STEPS

NOTE: END PIECE OVERLAPS
EACH END OF STEP

RISERS OF OUTDOOR
PLYWOOD OR 1" WOOD,
LENGTH AS DESIRED.

CUT 2 PIECES OF
OUTDOOR PLYWOOD TOGETHER
TO HEIGHT AND WIDTH OF STAIRS

ROT BLOCK 2" x 4"
KEEPS STRUCTURE OFF GROUND

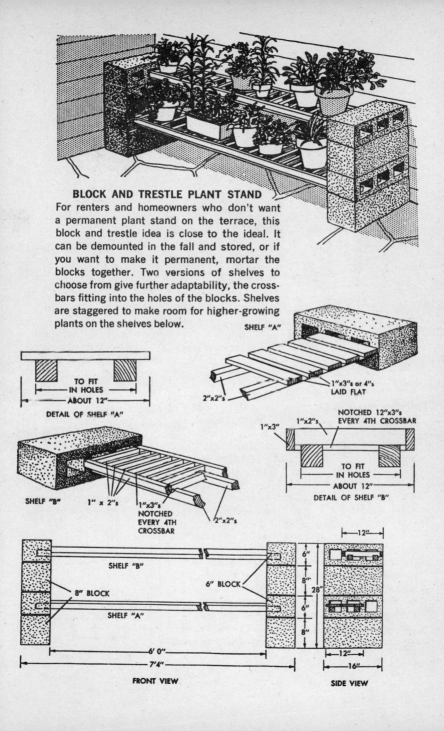

BLOCK AND TRESTLE PLANT STAND

For renters and homeowners who don't want a permanent plant stand on the terrace, this block and trestle idea is close to the ideal. It can be demounted in the fall and stored, or if you want to make it permanent, mortar the blocks together. Two versions of shelves to choose from give further adaptability, the crossbars fitting into the holes of the blocks. Shelves are staggered to make room for higher-growing plants on the shelves below.

SHELF "A"

1"x3"s or 4"s
LAID FLAT

2"x2"s

TO FIT
IN HOLES
ABOUT 12"

DETAIL OF SHELF "A"

SHELF "B"

1" x 2"s

1"x3"s
NOTCHED
EVERY 4TH
CROSSBAR

2"x2"s

NOTCHED 12"x3"s
EVERY 4TH CROSSBAR

1"x3"   1"x2"s

TO FIT
IN HOLES
ABOUT 12"

DETAIL OF SHELF "B"

SHELF "B"

8" BLOCK   6" BLOCK

SHELF "A"

6"
8"   28"
6"
8"

12"

6' 0"
7'4"

FRONT VIEW

12"
16"

SIDE VIEW

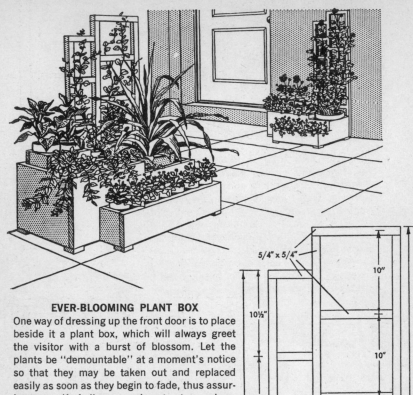

EVER-BLOOMING PLANT BOX

One way of dressing up the front door is to place beside it a plant box, which will always greet the visitor with a burst of blossom. Let the plants be "demountable" at a moment's notice so that they may be taken out and replaced easily as soon as they begin to fade, thus assuring yourself of all-summer beauty at your doorstep. Inexpensive to build—scrap lumber may be employed for most of it—the plant box features a series of tiers which allow the shoulders of the pots to rest on the box edges, giving good drainage and also support for the pots. The trellis shown may be used or not, made a bit taller or shorter, according to the plants you wish to use. Geraniums can be trained up on the trellis, or vining houseplants such as ivy or philodendron (if there is shade) or a pot of morning glories can be used. Paint the wood or stain it, according to what you prefer in the way of finish, but always use a good wood preservative over the entire surface of the box first, particularly on cut edges, then paint or stain it.

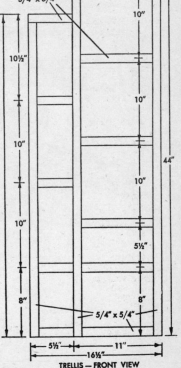

TRELLIS — FRONT VIEW

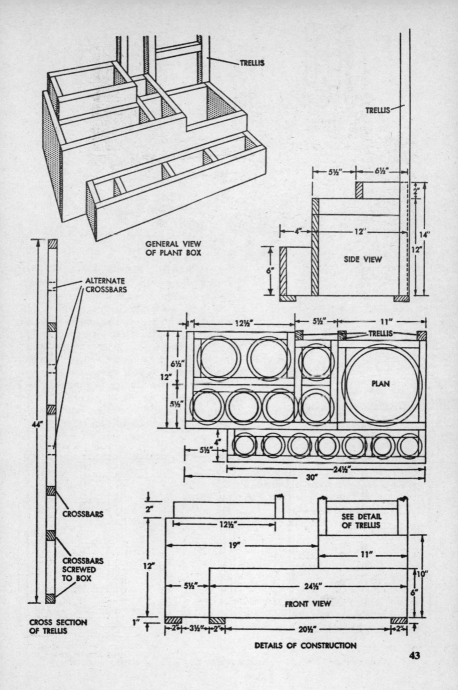

TRELLIS

TRELLIS

GENERAL VIEW
OF PLANT BOX

ALTERNATE
CROSSBARS

SIDE VIEW

5½"   6½"

2"

4"   12'

14"

12"

6"

44"

TRELLIS

PLAN

6½"

12"

5½"

1"

12½"   5½"   11"

4"

5½"

24½"

30"

CROSSBARS

CROSSBARS
SCREWED
TO BOX

SEE DETAIL
OF TRELLIS

2"

12½"

19"

11"

12"

5½"

24½"

10"

6"

1"

2" 3½" 2"   20½"   2"

CROSS SECTION
OF TRELLIS

FRONT VIEW

DETAILS OF CONSTRUCTION

43

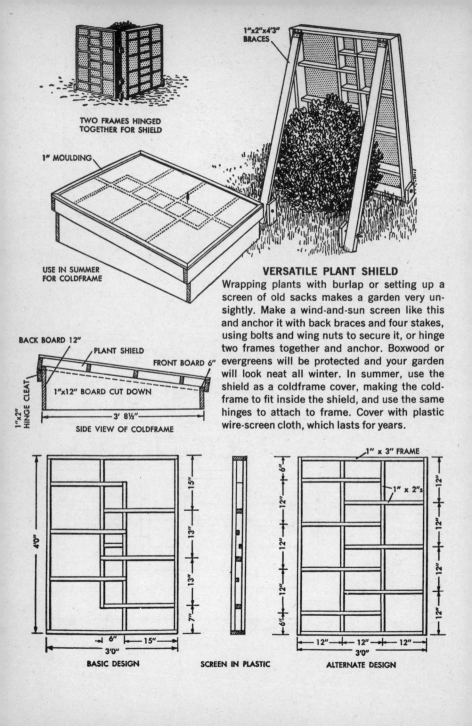

TWO FRAMES HINGED
TOGETHER FOR SHIELD

1"x2"x4'3"
BRACES

1" MOULDING

USE IN SUMMER
FOR COLDFRAME

VERSATILE PLANT SHIELD

Wrapping plants with burlap or setting up a screen of old sacks makes a garden very unsightly. Make a wind-and-sun screen like this and anchor it with back braces and four stakes, using bolts and wing nuts to secure it, or hinge two frames together and anchor. Boxwood or evergreens will be protected and your garden will look neat all winter. In summer, use the shield as a coldframe cover, making the coldframe to fit inside the shield, and use the same hinges to attach to frame. Cover with plastic wire-screen cloth, which lasts for years.

BACK BOARD 12"

PLANT SHIELD

FRONT BOARD 6"

1"x2"
HINGE CLEAT

1"x12" BOARD CUT DOWN

3' 8½"

SIDE VIEW OF COLDFRAME

15"

13"

13"

7"

4'0"

6"   15"

3'0"

BASIC DESIGN

6"

12"

12"

12"

6"

SCREEN IN PLASTIC

1" x 3" FRAME

1" x 2"s

12"

12"

12"

12"

12"   12"   12"

3'0"

ALTERNATE DESIGN

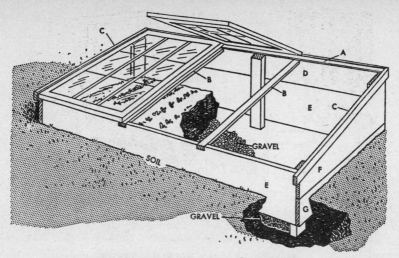

EVERY GARDEN CAN USE A COLDFRAME

For starting seeds early, for wintering-over tender plants, and for starting perennials in late summer, nothing can replace a coldframe. We recommend buying cypress sash already made up because they are relatively inexpensive; then build the walls to fit the sash. Sizes are usually: 2' x 4', 3' x 4', and 3' x 6', and come glazed or unglazed. For walls, cypress is preferred because it is long lasting; but other hardwoods may be used equally well if they are treated with wood preservative, replacing them in a few years if necessary; or walls may be built of concrete or brick with wood frame topping to hold the sash. Make a set of sash to fit frame, covering them with laths, to use when the weather warms enough to make shade desirable and glazed sash unnecessary. Propping block holds sash up at various levels for ventilation.

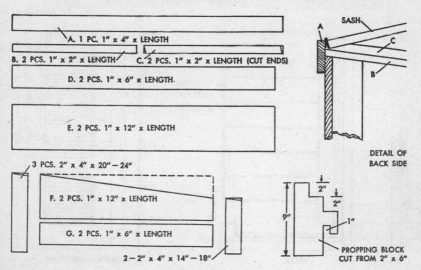

MAKE OVER UGLY DUCKLING DOORS

Old doors in bad condition or those which have panels of an ugly shape can be brought beautifully up to date. Cover them with a sheet of ½″ outdoor plywood with moldings framing shutter-effect panels made from overlapping trellis slats. Use a base of 1½″ doorstop molding, secured to plywood with waterproof glue and brads, a second molding on top overlaps slats ½″. Either high-crowned or flatter moldings may be used for the second one, depending on the effect desired. Bore holes of lock, knob, and cut slots for hinges if necessary. Use wood preservative before painting, fasten plywood to door with waterproof glue, or screws and nails of rustproof metal.

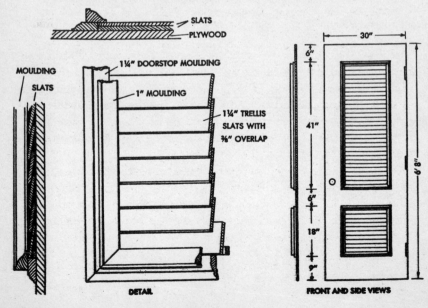

SLATS
PLYWOOD

MOULDING
SLATS

1¼″ DOORSTOP MOULDING
1″ MOULDING
1¼″ TRELLIS SLATS WITH ⅜″ OVERLAP

DETAIL.

30″
6″
41″
6″
18″
9″
6′ 8″

FRONT AND SIDE VIEWS

3

Every Garden Needs a Shelter

Today we find that the life of many a house has overflowed into the garden, making it a roofless outdoor room, so that the case for the need of a shelter is a good one. Most home owners will welcome some sort of shelter to add comfort to outdoor living. In moist climates they not only add a place outdoors in which to escape from sudden showers, but they also provide a place in which to sit of an evening and be protected from falling dew.

There are many shelters to choose from today. No longer need they be formally placed on the axis of the principal room of the house and have surroundings planted with overwhelming dignity, as in the past. Then the effect was impressive and beautiful but hardly invitingly cosy. Today's shelters are placed where they are *needed* and are usually casual and informal. Sometimes shelters will be found at the end of the garden, sometimes attached to the house, and sometimes freestanding along one side of the garden border—in fact, they will be placed wherever they are found to be most useful. They are practical, then, built for use as well as beauty. That is, perhaps, the outstanding thing about today's shelters that is universal.

Some of them bring a certain architectural significance to an ordinary development house, extending its lines and making it look larger, while giving it a distinctive appearance which divorces it from the factory-made appearance of its fellows on the street.

Sometimes the shelters are solidly roofed; sometimes they have crossbars for a roof (the so-called "egg crate" style); and sometimes they are roofed with laths or trellis slats, with sunbreakers of snow-fencing, or bamboo shades which can be rolled up in the autumn and stored indoors or in the garage during those months when light and warmth in the house are needed. Increasingly, however, you will find shelters becoming half-and-half structures—partly roofed and partly open or covered with sunbreakers. This will provide shelter from sudden storms under the roofed part, while the sunbreaker or open part will be pleasant for those who like the sun, either tempered a bit or full strength. Or it may be that the terrace paving will extend out beyond the structure of the shelter so that it is possible to move furniture into the sun when that is desirable and to pull it quickly under the sunbreaker or solid shelter when protection is wanted.

A revival of the old time gazebo seems to be taking place. These garden shelters were sometimes roofed, sometimes covered with slats or *treillage,* a crisscrossing of trellis slats that leave openings that are square, diamond-shaped, or oblong. There is much to be said for the gazebo—it is a pleasant and private place to retire to for a small gathering, to sit in and read or converse with a friend, to have a small luncheon or supper party of four or six, according to the size of the structure. In areas that are plagued with insects, the gazebo can be screened and a screen door fitted to give protection from these pests. An electric light

A garden shelter need not be elaborate—it may be as simple as you like. Consider this A-frame, made of redwood planks set in concrete embedded in the soil. Latticed roof uses 1" x 1" strips to shade the brick floor set on sand. Railroad ties form the rustic steps leading to it.

can also be installed so that one may enjoy the outdoors and summer cool in the evenings, as well as in the daytime. See photograph of a modern type.

In the designs herewith we have tried to provide a wide range so that you will find one which will harmonize with your house or which can be adapted to it. Even old houses are being brought up to date these days, with the addition of a garden house or shelter attached to the house or garage, or placed elsewhere in the garden, rejuvenating the whole site. A little remodeling of the garden to bring its plan up to date, to open it up, and to simplify it so that it is easier to take care of, and perhaps also the installing of a picture window to look out upon this garden-with-a-new-look, will help to make an old house more pleasant to live in as well as more saleable, should that necessity arise.

By taking into account your hobbies, your family life, your climate with its prevailing winds and other pertinent features, and the situation of neighboring houses, you can place your shelter where it will do the most good and add to your use of your garden, even improve your plants' chances for survival. For instance, if you live in areas where strong sun makes it difficult to grow camellias or other broad-leaved evergreens, you can give them the needed protection by placing your lath-roofed shelter so that its shadow is cast over adjoining beds. This will enable you to plant your favorites alongside your outdoor entertaining room, making a real conversation piece of this exhibit of your hobby plants.

By using a slat-roofed shelter, too, you will achieve privacy from above, where neighbors have second-floor windows overlooking your terrace or where a street or path overlooks it from a hill.

If you want protection from the eyes of observers but like to sit in the sun, the entire shelter need not be covered: part of it may be solid, another part slatted, and part of it left open so that you have three choices; and the divisions need not always be rectangular, either, but may be at an angle if you wish. Snow-fencing, bamboo, and basswood porch shades or roll-up blinds can also be used for slatting, being rolled up for storage in winter and held in place by 1" x 2"s or other light wood strips screwed in place on the shelter during the summer. This will prevent their being blown off or damaged by summer winds.

There is a preliminary consideration, however, which you must take into account. What do you need shelter from? Is it the sun, the wind, the prying eyes of neighbors and passersby? Once you have decided this question you will have a very good idea of where it would be best to place the shelter and what you will need in the way of screening.

Next you must decide on how permanent you want the shelter to be. Is it to be a freestanding one which will be a stand-in for a young tree still too small to give shade and visual privacy from upstairs windows or adjacent houses? A lightweight but well-built, sturdy structure would be indicated so that it would last until the tree took over.

Is it to be a really permanent shelter? Then there must be even more care given to its planning and construction so that it will withstand the stress of all-year weather and storms, and it should be well-designed so that it will be a permanent asset, a credit to both the house and the garden. Don't rush things at this point, for the shelter must stand the test of future years, which makes the preliminary thinking of primary importance. The permanent shelter should have permanent paving; its posts should be firmly embedded in concrete; and if they are of wood they should be treated with wood preservative before being set. All parts of wood structures outdoors will last indefinitely if they are thoroughly treated with wood preservative.

SIZE AND HEIGHT

In general, with today's homes being built long and low, it will be a good plan to echo these proportions in other structures. The average height of indoor rooms today is 8'0". Outdoor rooms may not *need* to be higher than that, particularly those with open or slatted roofs, but, architecturally speaking, most shelters attached to the house or another building look better when they have their roofs or trellises placed at, or just below, the eaves of the adjacent roofs, usually 9 to 10 feet above ground level. Attach the stringer enough below the line of the gutter so that crossbars or other superstructure may be placed on top and it will still come below the gutter. If this is too high, any normally visible architectural division of the house—the eaves of a low ell, the strong line of a tall picture window or door—may be your cue for placement. If not, then place the shelter so that the lower side of the rafters will clear the doors and windows by at least 6 inches or even a foot.

PLACEMENT OF POSTS

Similarly, in deciding on the placement of posts or other uprights, it is obvious that they should never be placed in front of a door or window to bisect it, obscuring the view of the garden from indoors or impeding direct entry into the house. It is also apparent that in attaching a shelter to a building it should not end inside the vertical lines of a window or a door opening, but should come at least to the edge or, better still, should extend beyond it by 6 inches or a foot, if possible.

Frequently there is an ell or a jog in the house wall which will make it convenient to place your shelter in the corner formed by the two walls, provided that this location will work out from the practical standpoint of use, and also that it will look well in the garden. If it gives you privacy and protection from wind, and if it is where its use at night will not disturb sleeping children or elder members of the family, you will find that the use of two existing walls will cut down on the labor required for building and also the expense of materials for construction, saving the cost of several posts and their setting. Jogs or breaks in roof lines also make good places to start or end shelters.

OTHER FEATURES

Frequently two or more useful functions may be combined in one structure. For instance, it may be possible that in building your garden shelter you will make a screen for a service yard where compost heaps, clotheslines, trash and garbage cans, and other un-beautiful but necessary adjuncts of modern life are congregated. This can be done by

A fanciful and pleasing octagonal garden shelter that is a modern descendant of the Victorian gazebo is open on two sides, windows are seen on two others and the slatted sides give it textural interest, provide climbing support for vines to give privacy.

merely adding a solid wall to the back of the structure, if it is free-standing in the garden, or else the wall may be backed up by a tool shed, an outdoor potting bench, or a garden storage house. The shelter wall may also be used as a place to display and shelter summering house-plants if shelves are built for the pots. They should be conveniently placed for necessary watering but also with an eye to showing off the potted plants in a decorative manner. The plants will thrive beneath a lath roof where they get enough light but are protected from the burning rays of the sun.

A shelter is a good play-place for children, too. With their vivid imaginations it can become a castle, a pirate ship, a prairie schooner, or the most modern of space ships. They can play in its shade all day long during the dog days when heat stroke stalks the open lawn. They will remember it with pleasure in adult years as a place where lunching and dining outdoors during the green seasons helped to knit the family together and make it a unit. When the children have gone to bed, it becomes a refuge for the adults on pleasant summer nights.

MATERIALS

In general, any wood which is used structurally in building houses may be employed for outdoor shelters.

Certain woods are favored because they are less susceptible to decay than others when used outdoors. Cedar, cypress, and redwood are the most prominent on the list, but almost any good, sound wood, well treated with wood preservative before it is painted, would last for many years if given yearly inspection and repaired and repainted as often as needed.

In some sections bamboo poles are cheap and available. They may be used as crossbars or set closely together as slats for view-breakers, or they may be used in conjunction with bamboo porch shades. It should be realized, however, that bamboo is not noted for its long-lasting qualities and that it will need periodic renewal. Reed mats, available through

A garden-house-gazebo of unique design is constructed throughout of long-lasting Western red cedar. Two-by-six posts are bolted to U-straps of steel set in concrete footings. Two-by-twos are centered on each side of the posts. Seats and backs are 2″ x 4″s; flooring, as well as framing, 2″ x 6″s.

nurserymen who use them as cold-frame coverings, are also available in many places. They may be used as view-breakers on fences or as shelter roofs, and may be rolled up and stored over winter. They do not cost very much, and it may be that their cheapness will make them attractive enough to compensate for their not lasting more than a few seasons.

Trellis slats in conventional 1½- to 2-inch widths, ¼- to ½-inch in thickness, will last for many years if painted and properly prepared. Cut the slats to size. A labor-saving device is to clamp a half dozen or more together and saw them all at once. Then unclamp them and stand them in a can containing about 4 inches of wood preservative. Soak the other ends too, letting them stand in the preservative for two to four hours or more; then remove them and let them dry well. Paint them with undercoat on all sides and ends and with a final coat of outdoor gloss paint. When that has dried install them on the trellis using aluminized or other non-rusting nails, and give the entire shelter a second coat of outdoor gloss paint, paying particular attention to filling well any joints or holes with paint. If there are any larger gaps, knotholes, etc., fill them with putty to prevent moisture from entering and then paint them. Use nails or screws which won't rust. This will preserve the shelter from rust stains and will cut down on the number of times it must be painted to keep it fresh-looking and to prevent further rusting.

SPARE THAT TREE

If one of your prized large trees should die, don't feel that you must immediately have it cut down. Instead, as demonstrated on a page of the designs for shelters, remove as many limbs and branches as may be necessary to prevent their breaking off or being blown off in storms and causing trouble. Plant a small tree nearby to give shade in future years, and then bolt long rafters of 2-inch lumber to the trunk of the dead tree (at least 2″ x 6″ lumber should be used), using 6- to 10-inch bolts to secure them. Keep rafters level and parallel to each other, using blocks if necessary to keep them equidistant. Eyebolts in the trunk at a distance of several feet above the rafters will hold cables to support outside corners of the structure. If you want to plant your new tree almost on the spot of the old one, support the middle of the rafters on the trunk and at the far end on posts.

A vine, either perennial or annual, or a combination of the two until the perennial vines grow large enough to mean something, will quickly cover the trellis and add shade-giving qualities, and will even climb the trunk and remaining limbs of the tree, preventing it from looking quite dead. Peeling the bark from the dead tree will prevent termites from doing too much damage to it. If you want to paint it a soft silver grey or a pale pastel color it can become a feature of your garden. Or, if you want to minimize it, paint it black or a soft dark green. Either way it will add distinction to your garden until the replacement tree is large enough. Then the shelter can be removed for its shade will no longer be needed.

To digress from the use of a tree as a shelter, perhaps you will want to use it in the following way if your dead tree has a picturesque shape which will compose well with a fence, a shelter, or some other feature: use it as a trellis for a vine. We have seen in this country large dead trees ablaze with wistaria bloom and, later in the season, feathery and lovely with the pale green leaves of that vine. In England and in the forests of France we have seen dead trees spreading their limbs in interesting patterns, their trunks and limbs clothed with the glossy leaves of ivy. It takes some years for ivy to grow that big, of course, and it won't grow in many places in this country; but other vines can be substituted, even annual ones, to make the dead tree a center of interest in the garden. At the base of the trunk a trellis may be built to support the vines and help them to reach the lower limbs.

USING YOUR SHELTER

Once your shelter is finished and planted with vines (if you have decided that you want such a leafy green roofing) you will begin to use it. We urge that you should not think of it as *finished*, however. As you use it, always be on the lookout for any way in which you can improve it, perhaps using some of the demountable coverings which we have advocated, perhaps developing some of your own methods of making sun- or view-breakers. Perhaps by hanging a roll-up blind on the sunny side of a necessarily small shelter you can outwit the broiling sun during the hot part of the day and then roll it up for evening or late afternoon.

But when your shelter has finally come to its completion and you are satisfied with it, enjoy it to the fullest and make the most of it. You will find that your new outdoor room has broadened and deepened the interest you take in your garden and in the outdoor living which it will make possible.

A TERRACE SUNBREAKER

Many picture windows are so placed that the glare of the sun cuts down their usefulness. A simple framework with posts securely placed on concrete and with the top rails attached to the house can hold snow-fencing, as shown here, which breaks the glare and heat in the summer and can be rolled up, stored in winter, when the sun will be welcome. Bamboo roll-up blinds, cut to fit, may also be used, or a more permanent trellis of slats, fiberglass, plastic aluminum screen, dowel rods, placed on basic frame.

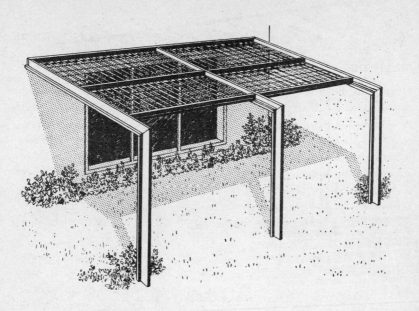

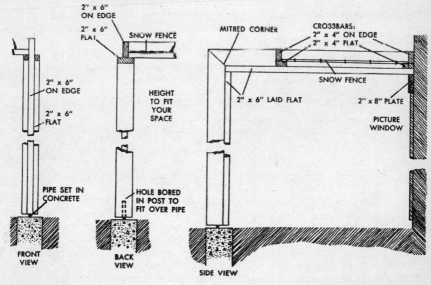

2" x 6"
ON EDGE

2" x 6"
FLAT

SNOW FENCE

MITRED CORNER

CROSSBARS:
2" x 4" ON EDGE
2" x 4" FLAT

2" x 6"
ON EDGE

2" x 6"
FLAT

HEIGHT
TO FIT
YOUR
SPACE

SNOW FENCE

2" x 6" LAID FLAT

2" x 8" PLATE

PICTURE
WINDOW

PIPE SET IN
CONCRETE

HOLE BORED
IN POST TO
FIT OVER PIPE

FRONT
VIEW

BACK
VIEW

SIDE VIEW

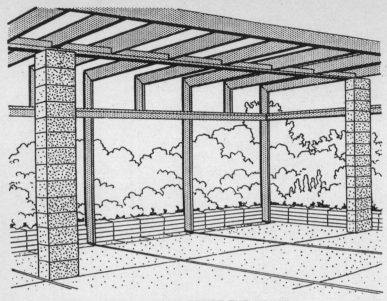

MAKE A TRELLIS ROOM BESIDE THE HOUSE

A good-looking and sturdy trellis covering a terrace alongside the house will add an outdoor room to your living space. Piers of blocks support the center stringer; uprights alternate full-length pieces with short uprights resting on the horizontal crossbar. A low plant bed constructed of flat blocks surrounds the terrace, giving further sense of enclosure. In our sketch, note that the back stringer is attached to the house, but it is possible to build a free-standing room by using upright construction on both sides.

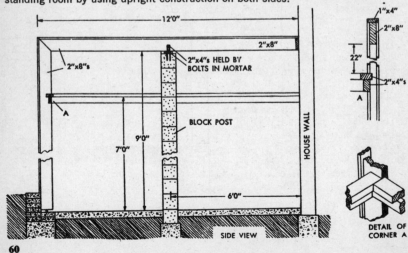

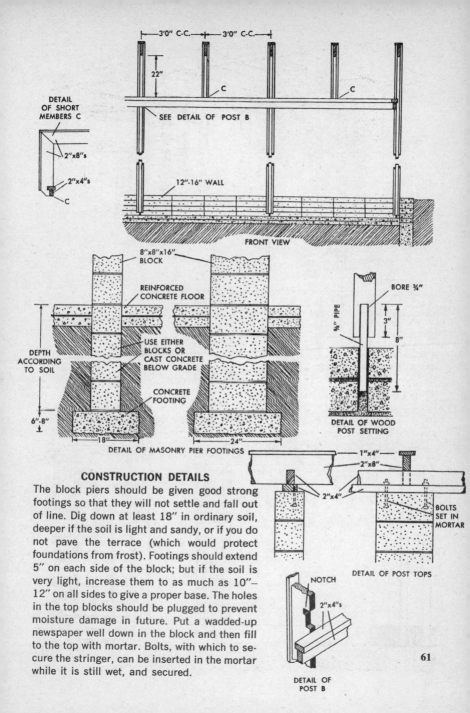

DETAIL OF SHORT MEMBERS C

2"x8"s

2"x4"s

C

3'0" C-C. — 3'0" C-C.

22"

C

C

SEE DETAIL OF POST B

12"-16" WALL

FRONT VIEW

8"x8"x16" BLOCK

REINFORCED CONCRETE FLOOR

USE EITHER BLOCKS OR CAST CONCRETE BELOW GRADE

CONCRETE FOOTING

DEPTH ACCORDING TO SOIL

6"-8"

18"

24"

DETAIL OF MASONRY PIER FOOTINGS

BORE ¾"

¾" PIPE

3"

8"

DETAIL OF WOOD POST SETTING

1"x4"

2"x8"

2"x4"

BOLTS SET IN MORTAR

DETAIL OF POST TOPS

NOTCH

2"x4"s

DETAIL OF POST B

CONSTRUCTION DETAILS

The block piers should be given good strong footings so that they will not settle and fall out of line. Dig down at least 18" in ordinary soil, deeper if the soil is light and sandy, or if you do not pave the terrace (which would protect foundations from frost). Footings should extend 5" on each side of the block; but if the soil is very light, increase them to as much as 10"–12" on all sides to give a proper base. The holes in the top blocks should be plugged to prevent moisture damage in future. Put a wadded-up newspaper well down in the block and then fill to the top with mortar. Bolts, with which to secure the stringer, can be inserted in the mortar while it is still wet, and secured.

61

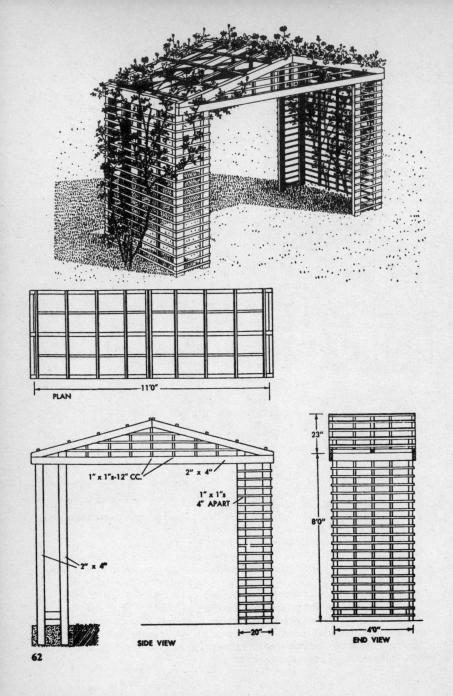

PLAN

11'0"

SIDE VIEW

1" x 1"s-12" CC.

2" x 4"

1" x 1"s
4" APART

2" x 4"

20"

END VIEW

23"

8'0"

4'0"

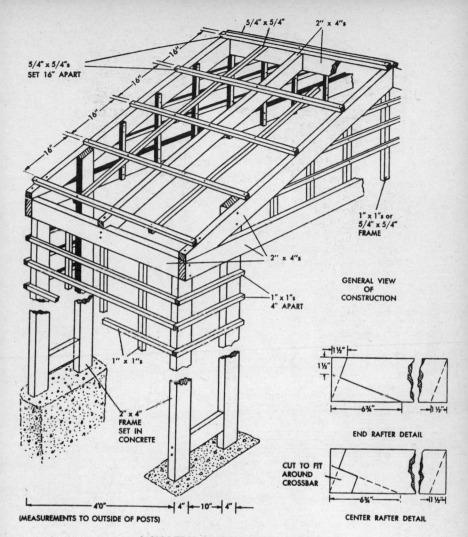

5/4" x 5/4"

2" x 4"s

5/4" x 5/4"s
SET 16" APART

16"

16"

16"

16"

16"

1" x 1"s or
5/4" x 5/4"
FRAME

2" x 4"s

GENERAL VIEW
OF
CONSTRUCTION

1" x 1"s
4" APART

1" x 1"s

1½"

1½"

2" x 4"
FRAME
SET IN
CONCRETE

6¾"

1½"

END RAFTER DETAIL

CUT TO FIT
AROUND
CROSSBAR

4'0"

4"

10"

4"

6¾"

1½"

(MEASUREMENTS TO OUTSIDE OF POSTS)

CENTER RAFTER DETAIL

A MODERN CLASSIC ROSE ARBOR

Adaptable to many uses, this arbor will go well with many traditional houses,
yet it has a modern flavor, too. It can be set in the open as shown here, used
in connection with a fence of similar design, be attached to a house or a
garage to roof a terrace, with suitable regard for harmonizing the roof lines
with those of the building. Its charm lies in the airiness of its proportions,
its form being geometric yet open enough to complement the wayward,
natural curvature of the climbing roses or vines, and at the same time sturdy
enough to bear their weight when, in future years, they will need firm support.
Use preservative on edges before painting.

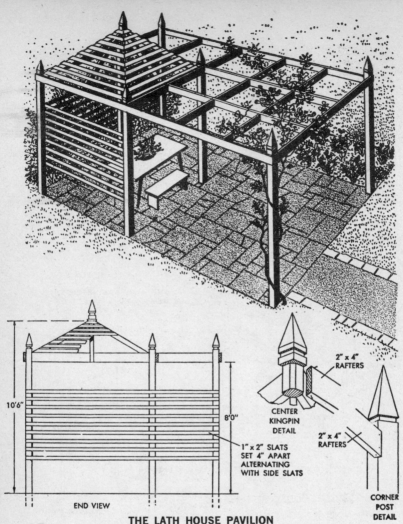

10'6"

8'0"

END VIEW

CENTER
KINGPIN
DETAIL

1" x 2" SLATS
SET 4" APART
ALTERNATING
WITH SIDE SLATS

2" x 4"
RAFTERS

2" x 4"
RAFTERS

CORNER
POST
DETAIL

THE LATH HOUSE PAVILION

A garden house which combines the better features of both the modern and traditional styles will give any garden a real focus as well as providing a useful outdoor living area. The corner "house" part is made more interesting by the use of 4" x 4" posts cut to taper to a point and rabbeted for decorative effect. The flat portions of the structure may be left open or roofed with laths, like the hip-roofed corner house. Note how laths are used on sides as viewbreakers and give privacy to the corner where they overlap. The entire area of the terrace under the structure may be paved, or only that under the house part, the rest being gravelled, or kept in lawn.

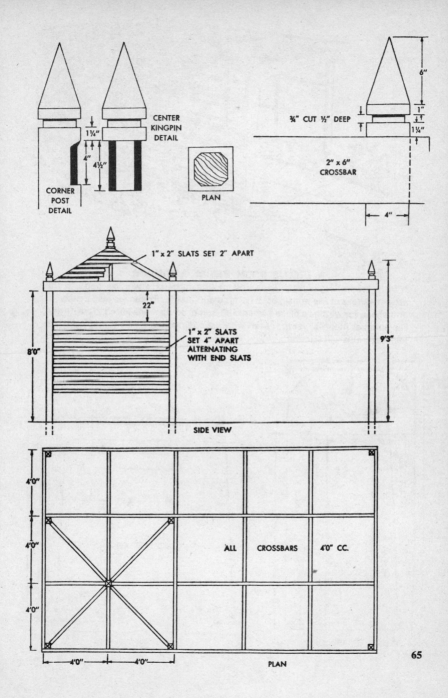

CENTER
KINGPIN
DETAIL

1¼"

4"

4½"

CORNER
POST
DETAIL

PLAN

¾" CUT ½" DEEP

6"

1"

1¼"

2" x 6"
CROSSBAR

4"

1" x 2" SLATS SET 2" APART

22"

1" x 2" SLATS
SET 4" APART
ALTERNATING
WITH END SLATS

8'0"

9'3"

SIDE VIEW

4'0"

4'0"

4'0"

ALL   CROSSBARS   4'0" CC.

4'0"   4'0"

PLAN

A TRELLIS ROOM BESIDE A WINDOW

A little "room" with leafy walls and ceiling outside a window adds to the attractiveness of the house, both outside and inside. Privacy is also achieved, and shade for windows placed where the sun produces unwanted glare during the summer months; yet in winter, when sun is needed for heat and light, the leafless trellis will admit it.

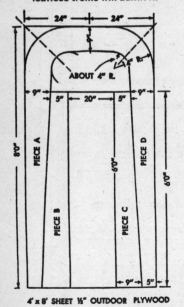

ABOUT 4" R.

PIECE A

PIECE B

PIECE C

PIECE D

4' x 8' SHEET ½" OUTDOOR PLYWOOD

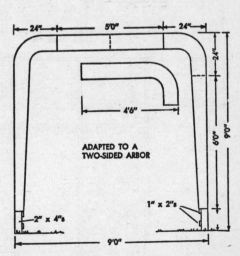

ADAPTED TO A
TWO-SIDED ARBOR

2" x 4"s

1" x 2"s

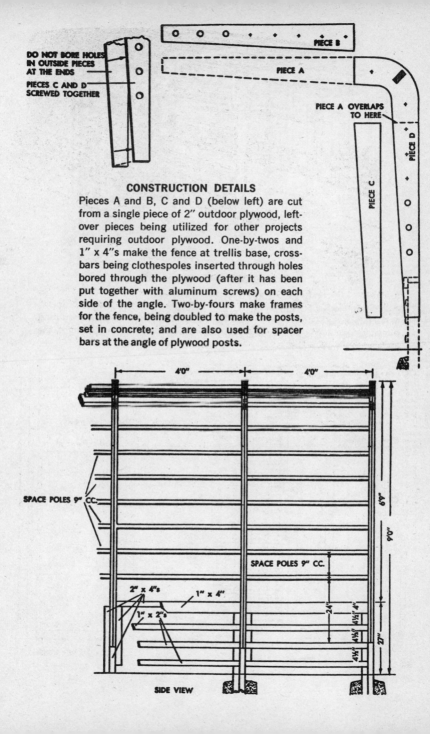

DO NOT BORE HOLES IN OUTSIDE PIECES AT THE ENDS

PIECES C AND D SCREWED TOGETHER

PIECE B

PIECE A

PIECE A OVERLAPS TO HERE

PIECE D

PIECE C

CONSTRUCTION DETAILS

Pieces A and B, C and D (below left) are cut from a single piece of 2" outdoor plywood, left-over pieces being utilized for other projects requiring outdoor plywood. One-by-twos and 1" x 4"s make the fence at trellis base, cross-bars being clothespoles inserted through holes bored through the plywood (after it has been put together with aluminum screws) on each side of the angle. Two-by-fours make frames for the fence, being doubled to make the posts, set in concrete; and are also used for spacer bars at the angle of plywood posts.

4'0" 4'0"

SPACE POLES 9" CC

6'9"

9'0"

SPACE POLES 9" CC.

2" x 4"s   1" x 4"

1" x 2"s

24"

4½" 4"

4½"

27"

4½"

SIDE VIEW

SLIDING SCREEN WITH BAMBOO

Bamboo porch shades are cheap to buy, can be fastened to basic framework as shown below (bosswood detail), finished off with moldings. When sun or more view is desired, screens slide aside easily on marbles in a rabbeted channel cut into the bottom piece.

DETAIL OF MARBLE TRACK

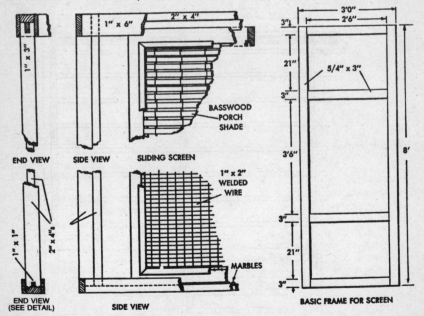

END VIEW

SIDE VIEW

SLIDING SCREEN

BASSWOOD PORCH SHADE

1" x 6"

2" x 4"

1" x 3"

END VIEW (SEE DETAIL)

SIDE VIEW

1" x 1"

2" x 4"

1" x 2" WELDED WIRE

MARBLES

3'0"

2'6"

3"

21"

3"

5/4" x 3"

3'6"

3"

21"

3"

8'

BASIC FRAME FOR SCREEN

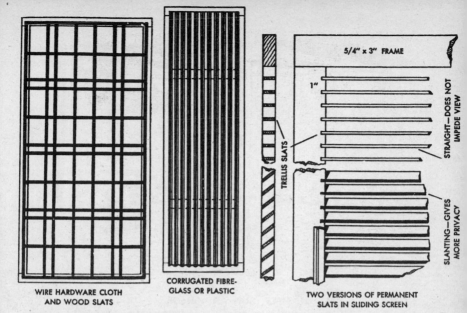

WIRE HARDWARE CLOTH
AND WOOD SLATS

CORRUGATED FIBRE-
GLASS OR PLASTIC

TRELLIS SLATS

5/4" x 3" FRAME

1"

STRAIGHT—DOES NOT
IMPEDE VIEW

SLANTING—GIVES
MORE PRIVACY

TWO VERSIONS OF PERMANENT
SLATS IN SLIDING SCREEN

SLIDING SCREEN FOR PRIVACY

Picture windows bring problems of privacy and frequently too much sun. One way to solve both problems is to use sliding screens mounted on a sturdy framework. They can be painted to contrast with or to match the house, stained or allowed to weather. Many materials can be used—bamboo or basswood porch shades, wire hardware cloth, trellis slats, snow fence, corrugated fiberglass or plastic—and many other coverings can be applied on the basic framework shown left. With bamboo and basswood shades, a groove should be cut deep enough to admit the shade, which is tacked to the frame and a molding applied to give a neat finish to the edge. With corrugated plastic, hardware cloth or wire, material can be stretched firmly over frame, molding applied on top if a finish is desired. An interesting new variation on the permanent slat idea is the horizontal slat set straight, which shades and does not impede the outward view, but breaks the inward view. Permanent slats can also be set at an angle, as seen in upper version. The molding gives a neat-looking finish to the da-doed slat inserts.

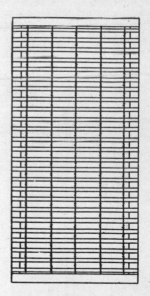

SNOW FENCE

69

HALF-AND-HALF, SUN AND SHADE

Roofed with a 1″ x 2″ trellis supported by a 2″ x 4″ frame and sturdy posts set in concrete, this terrace cover provides shade on hot days in summer, or warmth of the sun on cool days in spring and autumn. On two sides the neighbors are kept at bay by a raised fence faced with either Transite or plywood, louvers or spaced trellis slats.

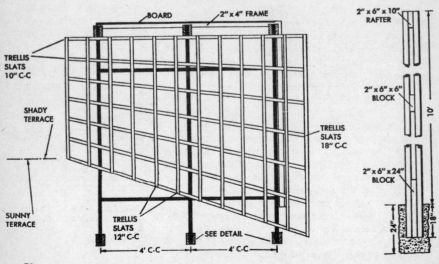

SHADE FOR WHEN A TREE DIES

Regrettable as the loss of a large shade tree may be, it needn't rob you of shade completely. It is possible to utilize the tree as a source of shade for some years more until its replacement grows big enough to contribute sufficient protection. Cut off all limbs and branches likely to be dislodged by the wind, then bolt the center 2" x 6"s to the trunk, then attach the 2" x 4" frame members securely and apply the trellis strips. For complete support, use steel cables through eyebolts to four corners. A wisteria or some other permanent vine planted at the trunk and trained up to cover the shelter will eventually clothe it and even the trunk and limbs of the tree.

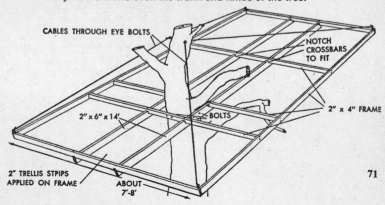

CABLES THROUGH EYE BOLTS

NOTCH CROSSBARS TO FIT

2" x 6" x 14'

BOLTS

2" x 4" FRAME

2" TRELLIS STRIPS APPLIED ON FRAME

ABOUT 7'-8'

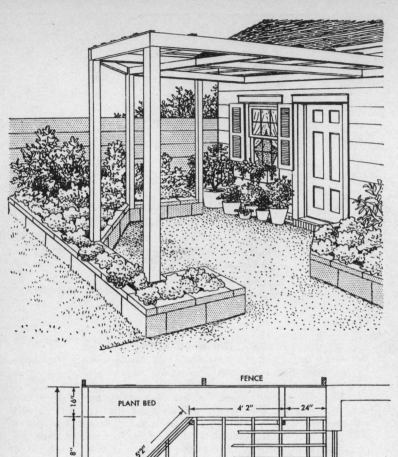

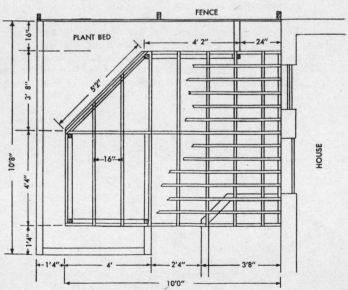

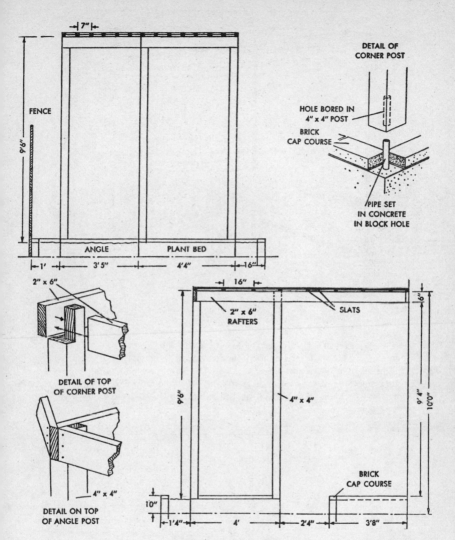

A NEW ANGLE ON TRELLISES

Even though a terrace is quite tiny, it can still have charm—in fact, the smaller it is the more it *needs* charm. An unconventional trellis which fits well with a traditional house, such as this one, lends piquance to the home scene. Blocks form a low plant bed, give year-round definition to the terrace which in summer is graced with potted plants; annuals are used with shrubs in the beds. The trellis breaks the sun's rays, providing a place for annual vines to climb on. The clapboard fence continues lines of the house.

73

AN EYRIE FOR EATING—OR DREAMING

Although shown as a platform extended over a declivity, this corner arrangement might be built equally well on the level. The seats are hung from the supporting members of the trellis, as is the table on one side. Outdoor plywood may be used for seats as well as the table top if a sturdy frame of 2″ x 2″s or heavier were used for support.

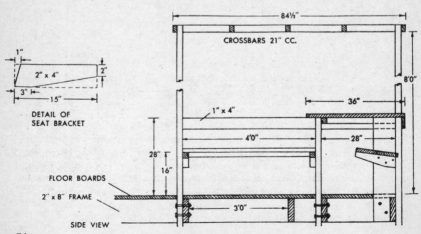

DETAIL OF
SEAT BRACKET

CROSSBARS 21″ CC.

FLOOR BOARDS

2″ x 8″ FRAME

SIDE VIEW

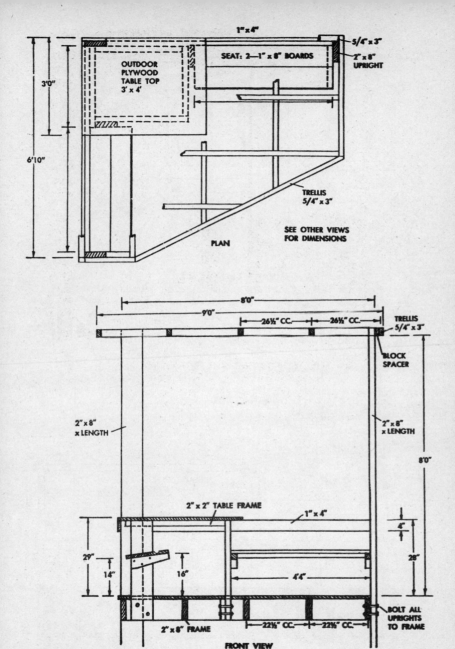

PLAN

1" x 4"

5/4" x 3"

SEAT: 2—1" x 8" BOARDS

2" x 8" UPRIGHT

OUTDOOR PLYWOOD TABLE TOP 3' x 4'

3'0"

6'10"

TRELLIS 5/4" x 3"

SEE OTHER VIEWS FOR DIMENSIONS

FRONT VIEW

8'0"

9'0"

26½" CC.

26½" CC.

TRELLIS 5/4" x 3"

BLOCK SPACER

2" x 8" x LENGTH

2" x 8" x LENGTH

8'0"

2" x 2" TABLE FRAME

1" x 4"

4"

29"

14"

16"

28"

4'4"

2" x 8" FRAME

22½" CC.

22½" CC.

BOLT ALL UPRIGHTS TO FRAME

A SHADOWPLAY SHELTER

This quadrangular shelter is a little off the beaten track, with its seat roofed over and its trelliswork casting shadows of ever-changing patterns on the gravelled terrace. It adapts itself to many kinds of gardens.

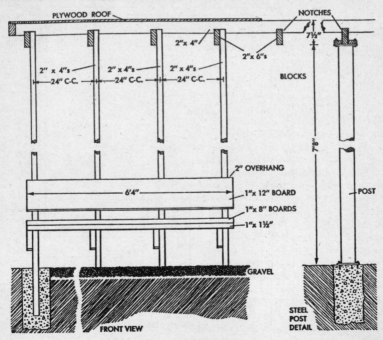

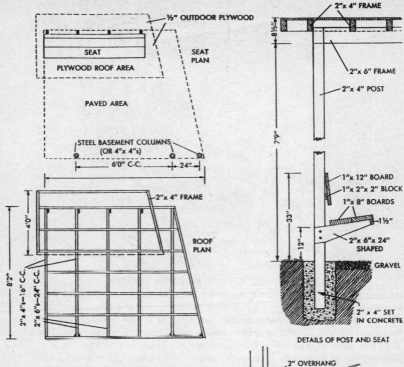

½" OUTDOOR PLYWOOD

SEAT

PLYWOOD ROOF AREA

SEAT PLAN

PAVED AREA

STEEL BASEMENT COLUMNS (OR 4"x 4"s)

6'0" C-C.   24"

2"x 4" FRAME

ROOF PLAN

4'0"

8'2"

2"x 4"'s—16' C-C.

2"x 6"—24" C-C.

2"x 4" FRAME

8½"

2"x 6" FRAME

2"x 4" POST

7'9"

1"x 12" BOARD
1"x 2"x 2" BLOCK
1"x 8" BOARDS
1½"

33"

12"

2"x 6"x 24" SHAPED

GRAVEL

2" x 4" SET IN CONCRETE

DETAILS OF POST AND SEAT

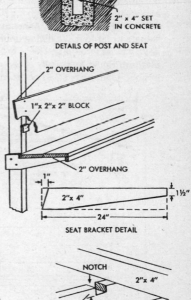

2" OVERHANG

1"x 2"x 2" BLOCK

2" OVERHANG

1"

2"x 4"

24"

1½"

SEAT BRACKET DETAIL

NOTCH

2"x 4"

1½"

2"x 6"

TRELLIS DETAIL

FURTHER DETAILS

Basically the shelter is simplicity itself, consisting of four upright wooden posts set in concrete on one side, supporting trelliswork and seat, while on the other side three steel basement columns, bolted to a concrete base, hold up the front, giving unobstructed views of the garden. Wooden posts (4" x 4") could be substituted if desired. Only the area over the seat is roofed over, either outdoor plywood or Transite being used, but both need sloping from front to back to provide quick drainage and thus preserve the roofing material. The 2" x 4" frame for the roof is notched to fit over the trelliswork frame, and nailed in place. Vines which climb on the trellis give adequate shade in the summer; and when they are leafless in spring and autumn, sufficient sun enters the trellis to make it possible to sit outdoors.

GARDEN HOUSE WITH A MODERN FLAVOR

Informality is the keynote of this structure with its seat along the back wall and the poles on the sides giving it strength and a feeling of enclosure without restricting outward view. Annual vines can clamber up the poles toward the shingled roof to make dining under cover a delight during the summer. The paving is set into the soil here, but a concrete or a brick- or stone-on-concrete platform would be equally acceptable. Similarly, in place of the dwarf trees in pots, plant beds could be let into the paving and made gay with annuals.

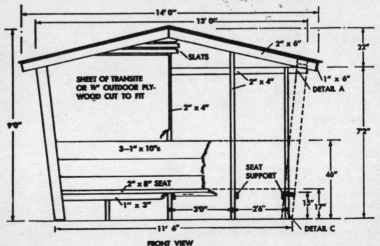

FRONT VIEW

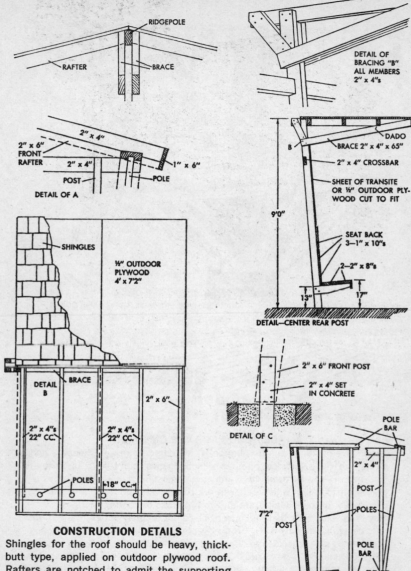

RIDGEPOLE

RAFTER — BRACE

DETAIL OF BRACING "B" ALL MEMBERS 2" x 4"s

2" x 4"

2" x 6" FRONT RAFTER

2" x 4"

POST — POLE — 1" x 6"

DETAIL OF A

DADO

BRACE 2" x 4" x 65"

2" x 4" CROSSBAR

SHEET OF TRANSITE OR ½" OUTDOOR PLYWOOD CUT TO FIT

B

9'0"

SEAT BACK 3—1" x 10"s

2—2" x 8"s

13" 17"

DETAIL—CENTER REAR POST

SHINGLES

½" OUTDOOR PLYWOOD 4' x 7'2"

DETAIL B — BRACE

2" x 6"

2" x 4"s 22" CC. 2" x 4"s 22" CC.

POLES 18" CC.

2" x 6" FRONT POST

2" x 4" SET IN CONCRETE

DETAIL OF C

POLE BAR

2" x 4"

POST

POLES

POST

7'2"

POLE BAR

SEAT SUPPORT

DADO INTO POST

CONSTRUCTION DETAILS

Shingles for the roof should be heavy, thick-butt type, applied on outdoor plywood roof. Rafters are notched to admit the supporting rails and the bracing members "B" are either nailed or bolted to post. Place 65" members first, then cut angle supports accurately to fit spaces, secure them to post and ridgepole.

DETAIL—RIGHT REAR POST—FRONT VIEW

79

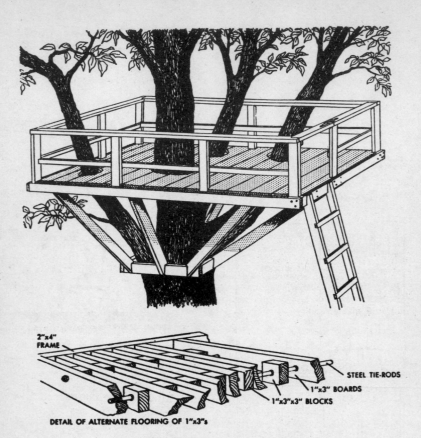

2"x4" FRAME

STEEL TIE-RODS

1"x3" BOARDS

1"x3"x3" BLOCKS

DETAIL OF ALTERNATE FLOORING OF 1"x3"s

A TREE HOUSE FOR THE CHILDREN

The first requisite of any tree house is, of course, the tree. Choose a good strong one with a sufficient number of limbs to give good solid support to the framework. Keep the frame as light as is consistent with safety (always the prime consideration where children are concerned) and brace the platform adequately. In the sketches are shown two types of flooring, either of which may be chosen. Note that the upright posts are securely bolted to the frame, rails being fastened by nails. Hinged "gate" rail is lowered when tree house is in use to prevent accidents. Adapt the frame to the limb structure, securing it to the trunk only—limbs are likely to wave about in the wind. Holes in floor permit them to move without endangering the platform. Crossbars are bolted to the tree trunk with 6" lag screws, braces being notched to fit over crossbars and nailed.

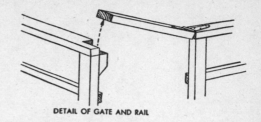

DETAIL OF GATE AND RAIL

FLOOR DETAILS

Conventional floor boards, 1" x 6" or 1" x 8", may be utilized, or ½" outdoor plywood laid on diagonal subflooring of rough or scrap lumber. Alternate flooring (left) may require more work but it will last indefinitely, making a right framework and providing perfect drainage in wet climates. Use 2" x 4"s for its outer framework, 1" x 3"s separated by 1" x 3" x 3" blocks, all bolted together with steel tie-rods through holes bored through boards and frame, giving rigidity.

CONTINUED▶

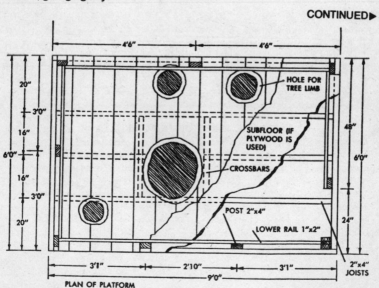

PLAN OF PLATFORM

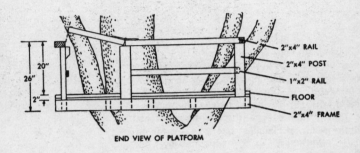

END VIEW OF PLATFORM

- 2"x4" RAIL
- 2"x4" POST
- 1"x2" RAIL
- FLOOR
- 2"x4" FRAME

26"
20"
2"

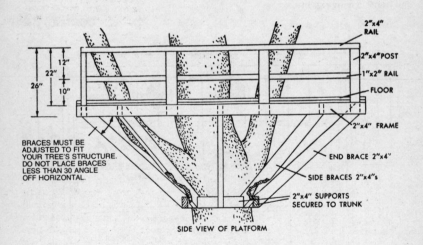

- 2"x4" RAIL
- 2"x4" POST
- 1"x2" RAIL
- FLOOR
- 2"x4" FRAME
- END BRACE 2"x4"
- SIDE BRACES 2"x4"s
- 2"x4" SUPPORTS SECURED TO TRUNK

26"
22"
12"
10"

BRACES MUST BE ADJUSTED TO FIT YOUR TREE'S STRUCTURE. DO NOT PLACE BRACES LESS THAN 30 ANGLE OFF HORIZONTAL.

SIDE VIEW OF PLATFORM

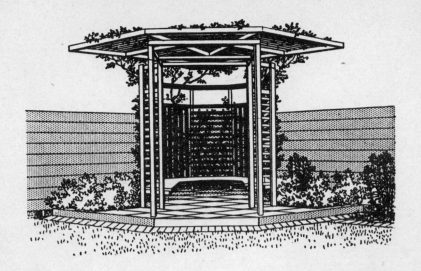

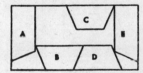

LAYOUT FOR CUTTING SEATS FROM
ONE 4'x 8' SHEET OF PLYWOOD.
LETTERS KEY SEATS TO PLAN BELOW

CONTINUED▶

ATTRACTIVE SHELTER IN A CORNER

A corner of a garden may create a most difficult problem in the small-home grounds. By using shiplap or scored outdoor plywood to give long lines to the fence and by echoing those lines with slats of the shelter, by using boldly opposing vertical lines to support the roof, we create a garden house both good-looking and unique. The seats add comfort and a place for dining, while the plywood part of the roof provides both sun and shelter.

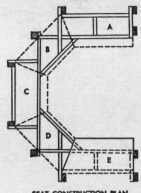

SEAT CONSTRUCTION PLAN

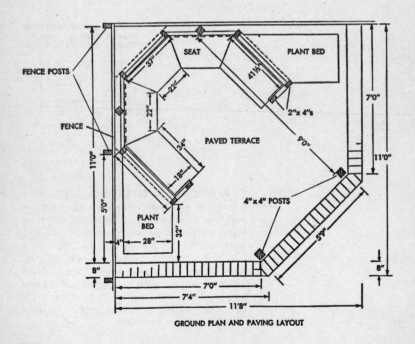

GROUND PLAN AND PAVING LAYOUT

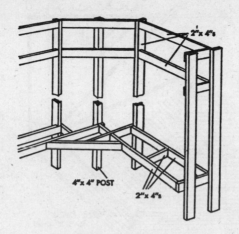

CONSTRUCTION OF FRAMEWORK

CONTINUED ▶

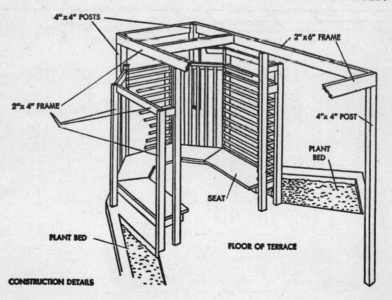

CONSTRUCTION DETAILS

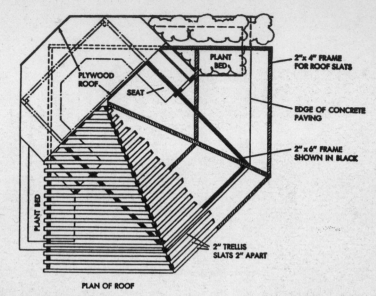

PLANT BED

2"x 4" FRAME
FOR ROOF SLATS

PLYWOOD
ROOF

SEAT

EDGE OF CONCRETE
PAVING

2" x 6" FRAME
SHOWN IN BLACK

PLANT BED

2" TRELLIS
SLATS 2" APART

PLAN OF ROOF

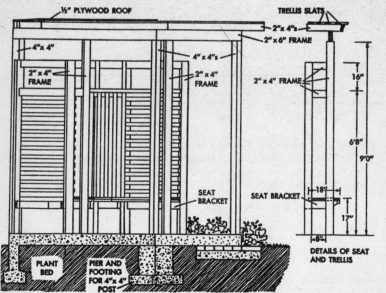

½" PLYWOOD ROOF

TRELLIS SLATS

2" x 4"s

2" x 6" FRAME

4" x 4"

4" x 4"s

2" x 4"
FRAME

2" x 4"
FRAME

2" x 4" FRAME

16"

SEAT
BRACKET

6'8"

9'0"

SEAT BRACKET

18"

17"

PLANT BED

PIER AND
FOOTING
FOR 4" x 4"
POST

8"

DETAILS OF SEAT
AND TRELLIS

A shelter with off-the-ground storage is built from exterior-type plywood on a sturdy wood frame. The 2" x 4" columns are firmly held by metal U-supports set in deep square concrete footings. Door shelves and hangers store small tools, supplies. Note slatted 2" x 4" seat.

Well integrated into a shelter and fence, a tool storage house built of grooved exterior ⅝″ plywood with interior grade inside in ¾″ and ¼″ thicknesses provides a place for everything needed in the garden and even a storage place for the barbecue between uses.

A garden storage house or a playhouse for the kids is designed like a barn and painted red. Built on a stout wood frame faced with Masonite Panel-groove hardboard (outdoor type) with pegboard inside for hanging tools and equipment, it is topped with wood shingles.

A neat and unobtrusive garden house has space not only for everything needed for entertaining outdoors but wide-opening front is composed of doors with door shelves similar to those on refrigerators that, with inside shelves, make furniture, dishes, implements available.

Everything under one roof in a triangular garden house: tool storage, potting shelf, even a tiny "greenhouse" taking advantage of waste space. A veritable gardener's dream. Framing is 2" x 4"s throughout; siding and roofing is Masonite exterior hardboard.

Drainholes are located in the hardboard floor. Glazed frames lift off.

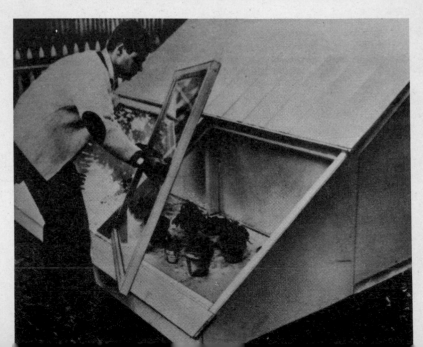

A flat-roofed exterior-plywood-covered storage unit houses not only the garden tools but also furniture and barbecue equipment, bicycles and other possessions. It even has a place for logs and refuse cans. Shaped built-up roof beams are made of doubled 2" x 8"s.

Who would think that what appears merely a pleasant jog in a fence could be a complete tightly-roofed tool storage house? The same boards and spacing of fence are used on 4″ x 4″ and 2″ x 4″ framing; padlocked doors keep everything safe.